thrifty*chic*

INTERIOR STYLE ON A SHOESTRING

thrifty*chic*

INTERIOR STYLE ON A SHOESTRING

LIZ BAUWENS AND
ALEXANDRA CAMPBELL

PHOTOGRAPHY BY SIMON BROWN

CICO BOOKS
LONDON NEW YORK

DEDICATION:
from Liz:
To my husband, Simon Brown, and my children, Lois, Milo, and Finn

from Alexandra:
To Freddie and Rosie.
love Alexandra

This edition published in 2017 by CICO Books
an imprint of Ryland Peters & Small Ltd
20–21 Jockey's Fields,   341 E 116th St,
London, WC1R 4BW   New York, NY 10029

www.rylandpeters.com

10 9 8 7 6 5 4 3 2 1

First published in 2009

A CIP catalog record for this book is available from the Library of Congress
and the British Library

ISBN 978-1-78249-497-3

Printed in China

Editor: Gillian Haslam
Text editor: Henrietta Heald
Designer: Christine Wood
Photographer: Simon Brown
Illustrator: Kate Simunek
Project text: Kate Haxell and Alison Wormleighton

contents

Introduction 6

introduction

The word "thrift" has become newly fashionable, but it also relates to real need. If you can't afford to furnish your home the way you would like to, you may also find that thrift can be inspiring. It forces you to look at things with a fresh eye: could that tatty old chest be painted up? Might that chair look better in a different fabric? Could you cut those faded curtains down into cushions? There's the joy of hunting around garage and car boot sales, auctions, junk stores, and even family attics, hoping to spot something that everyone else has missed, and there's also the pleasure of knowing that instead of consigning an old sofa or a battered table to a landfill site, you're making it live again.

And thrift isn't just about buying second-hand. Today's chain stores offer very affordable basics, often in good simple designs, which work in either traditional or contemporary homes. In addition, the seasonal sales, factory outlets, and the internet all offer excellent value for money. The key is to spend time scouting around, checking out prices and brands, and focusing your mind on what you really want. Never buy something just because it seems to be a bargain. Simplicity and neutral colors are the key to buying successful high-priced items, because you can dress them up and change their look with accessories.

The houses we've photographed for this book show that thrifty style doesn't have to look worn-out or threadbare: you'll find contemporary, classic, retro, modern, traditional, and eclectic interiors, all cleverly created on tight budgets by their owners, who have shared their tips with us. We hope you find the rooms on these pages as inspiring as we did.

elements of design

You don't have to spend a fortune to have a stylish home. It is the small details that make it special: the pretty window shade or the pillows and throws on a sofa or bed. If you are buying from chain stores, keep big purchases such as sofas, kitchen cabinets, and bathroom fixtures as simple and neutral as possible, then personalize your rooms by adding interesting accessories or imaginative decorative touches.

fabric

1 Keep your eyes open for vintage curtains that can be cut down to size to make delightfully retro substitutes for cupboard doors in kitchens, utility rooms, or even bedrooms and bathrooms.

2 For instant privacy, hang a length of voile or muslin over a line of wire. Peg in place with tiny clothespins.

3 Brighten up a pillow cover made in a plain fabric by sewing onto it decorative items such as buttons, patterns cut from other fabrics, or lengths of braid.

4 This boxy little chair was bought at a sale more than 20 years ago. Being a compact and classic design, it can be re-covered every few years in a different material at relatively low cost. Currently sporting a stylish floral fabric, this chair has also been covered at various times in hessian and in checks to go with different decor over the years.

5 Use small amounts of expensive fabrics—often available cheaply at sales—to cover bedheads or stools, and combine with other fabrics in similar shades and tones.

6 Look for vintage blankets or traditional plaids at garage or car-boot sales and on the internet. After being drycleaned, they will make perfect throws for chairs and beds.

paint

1 A basic piece of furniture bought from a thrift store or chain store can be transformed into something special by the application of paint. When painting large items, choose a color close to that of the walls, especially in small rooms. Many paint manufacturers offer groups of colors that are designed to work well together, or have created specific harmonies, so ask for guidance if you're not sure. Instructions for painting furniture are given on page 152.

2 Painting a floor is cheaper than any other floor-covering option, and white-painted floors reflect the light beautifully. Today's floor paints are hard-wearing and will stand up to at least a year of dirty feet tramping over them—many will last much longer. For instructions on how to achieve this painted staircase "runner," see page 154.

3 If you are decorating two adjoining or neighboring areas of your home that can be seen simultaneously through open doors, consider how their color schemes will look when viewed together. The "ice cream" tones used in these two bedrooms show how you can successfully combine completely different colors. Historic or "retro" colors are very suitable for paneled or tongue-and-groove walls.

4 The surface of this painted table is battered and scratched after many years of constant use, but it is still beautiful and its mottled surface will give no cause for worry about spills or stains. When you buy a piece of old furniture such as this, live with it for a while before deciding whether it needs painting or renovating at all—the patina of age has its own special charm.

windows

1 A rewarding decorating trick is to frame the view from your windows with a collection of decorative items. In this room, glass pebbles and stones have been carefully arranged along the glazing bars. Window style is important to the whole appearance of a building. If you have a historic or traditional home, try, if you possibly can, to retain the original windows. Replacing them with modern designs or standard double glazing will reduce the value of the property when you come to sell.

2 If it is not possible for someone outside to see in, there is no need for curtains—enjoy the view instead.

3 A transfer is an unusual and attractive way of maintaining privacy at a window without excluding too much light.

4 Hang an unusual object, such as a pebble, bead, or tassel, from the cord of a shade.

5 The ledge created where sash windows meet is a perfect place for displaying memorabilia. Garlands of dried flowers or shells can be hung from the lock.

frames

1 Center pictures above a piece of furniture such as a side table or sofa rather than spacing them across the whole wall.

2 Mix framed children's artwork with contemporary prints such as these by artists Terry Frost and Alice Mumford. Frame the children's art just as you would modern prints.

3 A vintage map of your area—hung in the kitchen or near the front door—makes an interesting picture and is helpful for guests planning to explore the area.

4 Old black-and-white photographs look great when framed on walls. Size makes a difference. Either use large photos or frame them with a large area of mount around the image.

5 Turn your stairwell into an art gallery, displaying anything from memorabilia to children's artwork, favorite prints, invitations, and old photos. Hang a mix of frames, mounts, and styles of picture—just crowd them together for the best effect. If the stairwell gets direct sunshine, avoid hanging watercolors, since these will fade in the sun. Gray, white, and yellow are all good background colors.

lighting

1 Chandeliers look spectacular in modern rooms and are now available at all price levels. To keep the cost down, buy a cheap chandelier and paint it with metal paint to give it a visual lift.

2 Transform an old bottle into a lamp using a smart contemporary shade. Electrical-goods stores sell specialized light fixtures for bottles, vases, and candlesticks; many of these have a discreet trailing flex.

3 This unusual lampshade, resembling clusters of white roses, was bought at a craft fair—these are often good sources of unusual items or hand-made items.

4 Festive lighting can look effective at any time of year. Hang a light wreath on a wall or mirror or string fairy lights along the top of a bookcase.

doorknobs

1 Changing the knobs can transform a cheap closet or chest of drawers. Knobs don't even have to match. Look out for unusual knobs in homeware stores or when on your travels— they're so easy to take home.

2 Drape necklaces or ribbons over doorknobs to achieve a bohemian effect.

3 Pick up antique handles from architectural salvage yards or garage or car-boot sales. If you are throwing away furniture that is beyond repair, consider saving the handles.

4 A floral-patterned china drawer knob adds charm to this enamel-topped kitchen table.

china and glass

1 British designer Lou Rota searches out china plates like these at secondhand sales and auctions, then adds her signature "bug" designs, turning everyday items into something unusual and collectable.

2 Collections of everyday objects can be beautiful and very cheap to build up. Here, a row of blue and green glass bottles makes an eye-catching display on a window ledge. Position glass items where the sunlight can enhance their beauty.

3 Displayed on these open shelves are tin plates, which can be found in many museum stores. They are as elegant as china (and look very similar from a distance) and much less likely to break. The "spot" mugs are from vintage design specialist Cath Kidston.

4 Pressed-glass items such as these pretty and elegant cakestands can often be found in thrift stores and at auctions. If you are interested in collecting specialty items, do your research in advance—it's easier to spot a bargain if you know what you're looking for. Use them to serve cakes for a traditional afternoon tea, to showcase collections of smaller items, or simply display them as objects of beauty in their own right.

5 A miscellaneous collection of quirky glass vases and candlesticks makes an impact on a marble mantelpiece. It's far cheaper to pick up odd candlesticks rather than pairs; if you adhere to a theme—such as glass, wood, bronze, silver, or china—they will all look good together. This collection works well as although all very different, each item stands tall.

mirrors

1 Small mirrors can be picked up cheaply at sales, auctions, and factory outlets. They improve the illumination in a room when hung together on the wall, and you can mix vintage mirrors with chain-store buys. All these mirrors, apart from the circular cream one on the far right, have "beveled edges" rather than frames; this look was popular in the first part of the 20th century, so you are more likely to find these secondhand than new.

2 Antique mirrors are now very sought-after, but it's worth making the occasional big investment to create impact. Don't be tempted to replace old glass with new, however tarnished it is, or you will alter the character of the mirror completely.

3 A charming thrift-store mirror hangs above a basic white china sink obtained from a plumbers' merchant. Hanging a mirror is not only a cheaper option than attaching sheets of mirror glass to the wall but also adds warmth and character to a bathroom. When installing a mirror in a bathroom, remember that people's heights vary.

4 Large mirrors are heavy to hang on walls—one alternative is to prop them up on the floor. If you put your mirror on the floor, check that it is secure. You don't want it to fall over if someone accidentally bumps into it. Huge mirrors work well in both modern and traditional interiors.

5 This simple chain-store mirror has been transformed by the application of a coat of paint, whose color echoes the other shades of gray in the room. When you are hanging a mirror, always check to see what it will reflect—the reflection of a charming chandelier or an attractive wall opposite is much more desirable than that of an ugly view outside or a part of your house you don't want to emphasize. More appealingly, you can "double" your view of your garden by hanging a large mirror near or opposite the window.

display

1 When creating mantelscapes and tablescapes, try to find a unifying theme. The items that make up this composition are linked by the theme of roses. There is a fresh rose in a chunky little vase, the cherub statue is holding roses, and at his feet is a row of china roses.

2 Practical items can form part of a display in a dining room. Everyday glasses are stored in the hanging cupboard, which came from an antique store, the candle is ready to be lit, and the oranges are waiting to be eaten.

3 This classical display has a theme—everything is connected with Napoleon. The theme brings together a collection of disparate objects, as does the limited color palette of silver, black, white, and gray.

4 Hooks attached to a piece of garden trellis, painted to match the wall, offer a cheap and stylish way to display and store kitchen utensils.

flowers

1 Dried seed heads, grasses, and pods from the garden last a long time and look attractive in the fall and winter, when fresh flowers are expensive.

2 Everyday items can be turned into planters and vases. Here, a can with its label removed makes a stylish small pot and an enamel jug is a useful vase.

3 If you enjoy having fresh flowers in your home every week but don't have much money, either buy two or three stems from a florist or snip a few from the garden. If you grow cut-and-come-again flowers, you will have blooms for your home all summer long.

4 A bunch of identical blooms looks more contemporary than a mixed collection of flowers.

5 Putting single flowers in individual but identical containers is a modern way of displaying just four or five blooms.

nature collections

1 Collections of pebbles are free and available everywhere. Line them up on a windowsill so that each one can be held and admired, or wash them and use on the dining table, French-style, to balance the tips of your knife and fork on between courses when you don't want to provide clean cutlery for each course.

2 Driftwood, fir cones, shells, and smooth pebbles are collected together and displayed on a wooden table. Group found objects together in categories for maximum impact: shells in one bowl, small pebbles in another, and so on.

3 Shells in a box can be used as an atmospheric desk tidy: a large beautiful shell is so much more attractive than a paperweight.

4 Paint a design on large pebbles or stones, then use them for paperweights, door stops, or just as ornaments.

5 Old-fashioned wooden clothespins, bleached almost white by the sun, make a charming companion collection to a plate of pretty shells collected on seaside walks.

halls and entrances

Your front door is the first introduction that guests have to your style, and it is not expensive to ensure that people are greeted with an attractive front door, polished door furniture, and a welcoming hallway. Hallways may be practical, with rows of hooks or useful shelves for unopened mail, coats, and boots, or they may be the home's art gallery, with pictures and mirrors. Or they can easily be both.

first impressions

Front doors—and back doors, too—reveal your personal style to the world. Hallways invite people in and promise them fun, grandeur, bohemianism, comfort . . . whatever image you want to project. Fortunately, entrance areas are usually relatively small, and people pass through quickly, so you can afford to make a dramatic statement without spending a fortune. Front doors, in particular, say a great deal about who you are, whether that is modern, traditionalist, country-at-heart, a fashion diva, or an architectural perfectionist.

When planning the decorative scheme for an entrance hall, remember that every time someone opens the front door the wall color and the light in the hall will change. Rooms leading off the hall should also be taken into account. Internal doors onto halls are often left open, so consider how your color choices for the hall will either harmonize or contrast with those of adjacent rooms.

left When the door opens, light is reflected in a group of mirrors on the wall, brightening up the space. Small mirrors such as these can be picked up cheaply and their wooden frames painted.

right The areas near the front door and back door can be used for storing boots and other useful objects, but there is no need to build cupboards to hide things away—there is often great beauty to be seen in rows of simple, everyday things.

left A wide windowsill can be treated like a mantelpiece. Here, a line of colored bottles makes a thrifty but fascinating "windowscape." Curtains are not generally needed on a landing, because there are rarely issues of privacy to worry about.

stairway style

It is common to identify the kitchen as the heart of the home, but in some ways the staircase also has a claim to the title. Winding up through a building's core, a staircase can pull everything together and make the house "flow" better both visually and practically. Halls and stairways usually have large expanses of wall—perfect for groups of paintings or family photographs—or the space can be used to display collections: favorite hats, children's artwork, anything that can be framed. "Crowding it up" is an old decorator's trick to make cheap items look special—a display of several plates is more effective than two or three, and in the hall no one will notice if they are chipped or slightly cracked.

Deciding to collect something specific will give you a focus for your visits to secondhand stores and garage or car-boot sales. Vintage packaging or magazine covers, old posters and postcards, even letters, menus, or other memorabilia—any of these can be framed to create a very personal, inexpensive montage.

right When decorating a landing, it is worth taking account of the views through and beyond, but that doesn't mean doing anything expensive—you can leave a hall or landing entirely empty and spend the money elsewhere.

color in hallways

When a door is opened onto a hallway, the color and atmosphere of the space change, as shown on these pages. With the bathroom door closed, the color scheme is elegant and calming, but when the door is opened, a blast of bright blue creates an effect similar to that of hanging a dramatic painting. You could turn this idea around, choosing a strong color for your hall and neutrals for the main rooms. Light can vary enormously from one part of a hall to another, so try out your chosen colors both near the window and in the darker areas. When thinking about hanging pictures or choosing lighting in a room, remember that you will also be seeing these objects from the hall, through an open door. In this case, the twin red splashes of the lampshades make a link between the two spaces.

above and left The elegant gray landing walls look quite different depending on whether the door is shut (above left) or open to reveal the rich blue of the bathroom (opposite). They look different again when a door is opened onto a neutral color (above).

above left A wide range of chandeliers is available, not only in antique stores and at auctions, but also in inexpensive chain stores. Choose a pretty shape and personalize it by painting it or adding strings of glass beads.

stairs and storage

Stair carpet can be one of the most expensive elements of decorating a hall but a painted "runner" will give you the same fashionable look for a fraction of the cost of the real thing. Mark out the lines of the stripes with masking tape before painting them. If you have a stairway that curves, you will need to settle for a relatively simple pattern. Floor paints are much more hardwearing than they used to be, and painting a floor yourself is clearly the cheapest option. If you are worried about wear, try yacht varnish. However, if you do decide to have a carpet, make sure it is suitable for stairs; very cheap carpet on a staircase can be dangerous because it is likely to be slippery at the lip of the step.

When storage is limited, halls and landings can offer valuable extra space. A simple row of hooks, a shelf, or a narrow chest or console table can make all the difference. The space under the stairs is a traditional place for storage, but make the most of every spare inch by installing shelves or inset wine racks; don't let it deteriorate into a glory hole where nothing can be found.

far left and above left A painted "runner" is much cheaper than real carpeting but looks very effective. Allow at least 24 hours for each stripe to dry out before painting the next one. See page 154 for painting instructions.

left Exploit every inch of understair space by customizing storage. You can make a wine rack such as this from a stack of small shelves. For the front, cut round holes in a strip of ply or MDF.

right Get inspiration for your pattern from a piece of fabric such as a scarf or a traditional ticking.

above right If the stairs curve, you will need to simplify the arrangement of stripes.

kitchens and dining rooms

Whether you are starting from scratch or trying to adapt an existing room, the kitchen and dining area are likely to absorb a large proportion of your home improvement budget. This chapter shows you how to make the most of what you've got, install a designer kitchen at a discount price, or make a kitchen from planks and bricks— as well as how to create dining spaces that complement your style of kitchen.

starting from scratch

The kitchen featured on these pages has been completely remodeled and renovated, making the most of a small budget, but it resembles something you might expect to see in a glossy magazine for three times the price.

Some works—architectural alterations and lighting installations, for example—have to be carried out professionally, and it is not advisable to cut corners on these items. In this kitchen, the window was made larger and the room was rewired to provide downlighters and wall lights. The good-looking stove is a reliable rather than a luxury brand.

Money was saved on the kitchen cabinets, the floor, and the storage. You can buy the basic cupboard units from home-furnishing chain stores. Here, a Shaker design has been decorated in a specialist historic white paint and paired with a stylish marble countertop. Although it may seem strange to spend more on the countertop than on the units, this is an effective way to make a chain-store kitchen look special.

Save money and space by installing open shelves above the counter. Cheap everyday items, such as a copper pipe, a drying rack, and garden trellis, have been adapted for hanging cooking utensils, and the floor has been scrubbed and treated to give it a bleached Scandinavian look.

left Keeping cabinets and large items such as a microwave oven below the counter increases the sense of space. The unit to the left of the sink is a slide-out trashcan that's also used for making compost. The marble countertop was sourced from a marble wholesaler.

top right Cooking equipment is stored on an old-fashioned drying rack hung from the ceiling.

center right A length of copper piping, bought very cheaply from a local plumber's merchant, is attached to the wall behind the cooker for hanging utensils.

right The chunky shelves are make from scaffolding boards supported by iron brackets—you can often find good-quality iron brackets in architectural salvage yards.

left Mismatched chairs, thrift-store purchases, and a pretty oilcloth make this kitchen seem friendly and welcoming, but there is a strong underlying sense of design; note the unusual wall clock and the gooseneck wall lamp.

below Old jars, cans, and mugs make good storage for pens, crayons, and scissors. Wicker furniture looks good when slightly battered. If you want to paint it, use acrylic paint as the wicker's flexibility makes latex or emulsion paint crack.

below right The big investment in this kitchen was the industrial-style faucet or tap, which comes with its own hose. It has a powerful spray for cleaning sink and surfaces.

Shown here is the dining area of the kitchen illustrated on pages 40–41, which has been furnished with a combination of purchases from auction sales, markets, and secondhand stores. The classic wooden chairs are not difficult to find, and you can collect them in ones or twos. If you have the time and the inclination, you can strip down old wooden chairs like these and repaint or revarnish them to make them match, but weathered paint and mismatched chairs inject a warmth into a kitchen that can offset the coldness of large modern appliances such as microwave ovens and refrigerators. You can disguise a table you don't like by covering it with an oilcloth tablecloth, which can be wiped down between uses—so buy the least expensive table of the right size you can find. A wicker sofa will look just as good in the garden as inside your home.

french-inspired

The combination of contemporary styling and French antiques is a very charming one, as exemplified by the kitchen shown on these pages. Basic items include a standard cooktop, wall oven, and kitchen unit, but there is one big indulgence: a hardwearing Corian countertop, which still looks good after 20 years of use. Added to these are the owner's collections of furniture and china picked up in flea markets, antique shops, and thrift stores, and on foreign trips.

Since one person's junk is another person's joy, friends can be a marvelous source of secondhand treasures. The set of cream shelves on the wall was rescued from a friend's clear-out, and has been installed on the wall above the cooktop, effectively distracting the eye from the practical element of the kitchen. This sort of arrangement can pose a fire risk, however, so check the maximum height and reach of any flames before installation.

above left These delightful storage jars were picked up in a Paris flea market. If you are on vacation in Europe, you can get details of local markets from tourist information centers.

left The Corian counter was an expensive investment 20 years ago—but its pristine appearance demonstrates that it is frequently worth spending extra on something that will last.

right The wood and metal chairs were made by a French artisan furniture-maker in Provence, and the table is also French, although it was bought at a London antique market. The china on the open shelves, collected over many years, is also mainly French in origin.

left A 1930s kitchen has been successfully updated and painted white. New white tiles behind the stove look crisp and modern. The furniture started life in the garden; having been well weathered outside, the teak table is also hardwearing in the kitchen.

below For a calm look, choose white; even the wicker flatware basket has been painted.

below right You can create a hutch or dresser effect with open shelving: items on display here include Victorian dessert molds and a collection of tin plates and spotty mugs.

far right The pantry area has been preserved exactly as it was, except for the addition of economical white tiling.

country cool

In the late 20th century it became customary to install a new kitchen when you bought a new home, but now people are saving enormous sums of money by making the most of what they've already got. In this case, the paneled tongue-and-groove cupboards date back to the 1930s, but they look charmingly fresh today when simply painted white. Painting cabinets the same color as the walls "loses" them—which is a good trick to know if you don't like the style.

The shelves above the cabinets in this kitchen are also original, but if you are remodeling a built-in kitchen, consider installing open shelving of a similar design. Shelves are less expensive than wall units and they make a small or narrow kitchen look more spacious because they don't protrude so far into the room.

new casual dining

Traditional dining rooms were distinguished by large and expensive items of furniture—an elegant period dining table with matching chairs, for example. Today's more relaxed lifestyle means that, when entertaining, we have come to regard the food and the company as more important than the furniture—and as a consequence our dining rooms are often prettier and more welcoming than their predecessors.

If you are lucky enough to have unusual architectural features in your home—or great views—keep the furnishings as simple as possible to show them off. As far as this house is concerned, the sea outside is the focal point of interest and has been an inspiration for the decorative scheme.

right The simple lines of the Arts & Crafts chairs are appropriate for the country setting and paneled tongue-and-groove walls.

below This chest was bought at the same time and from the same store as the table below left. While it's worth visiting thrift stores regularly to look for bargains, it can also be helpful to set yourself a deadline ("I need to buy a table this weekend") since this will encourage you to take risks.

below left A photograph by the owner's sister is framed above an enamel-topped table bought in a secondhand store. Old-fashioned telephones can still be bought cheaply.

cosmopolitan eclectic

This inviting dining room is in a city house but has a relaxed country atmosphere, created by the addition of objects from foreign countries, acquired during the owner's travels. Occupying pride of place is a battered table from a store specializing in Normandy furniture. It is perfect for family life because its surface is already so marked and layered with paint that it doesn't matter what children (or adults) do to it. The curtains were bought secondhand and altered to fit the window. The large chest of drawers had been left in the house by its previous owners; made of dark brown wood and adorned with fretwork and brass handles, it was transformed by having its embellishments removed, its handles changed to plain wood, and being painted cream. You can play about with furniture you've paid little or nothing for—it's amazing what a coat of specially formulated "historic" white paint can do. Other items were found in thrift stores and flea markets around Europe.

left A gilded flea-market mirror looks all the better for its tarnished antique glass—it can be a mistake to replace silvered or aged-looking glass, because modern mirrors are harsh and unforgiving. Hanging lampshades similar to the one seen here are available in home-furnishing chain stores.

below There are little vignettes on table tops all around this house—just four or five objects arranged to look pretty. Since the furniture is simple and the walls relatively bare, the effect is never cluttered. Many items, such as plant pots and candlesticks, are practical, too.

below center A glass-fronted chest from a market in Madrid has been hung on the wall above a tin table from a brocante in France.

below right An unusual cushion brightens up a classic kitchen chair.

left Steel handles add a stylish touch to basic chain-store units, while cheap white tiles make an impact when laid in a brick pattern. The wall tidy by the window is a modern design classic.

above right These attractive glass lights look effective in a row of three.

above far right The palette of steel, glass, and the colour white extends to pepper and salt grinders, storage jars, and olive-oil bottles.

below right This cabinet was made to the designer's specifications, using inexpensive elements such as flyscreen from a hardware store for the inset part of the doors.

urban cutting-edge

"Thrifty style" is not a narrowly defined look. It can appeal as much to those who want a sharp, contemporary edge to their home as to more traditionalist types. For example, interior designer Clare Nash created this steel-and-glass urban kitchen on a limited budget. She used chain-store units, utilitarian white tiles, and a steel counter cut to the right size by a steelworking company more used to dealing with businesses than individuals.

A controlled color palette and clever use of modern materials are what make this kitchen appear expensively cutting-edge. The use of wood and color is kept to a minimum and there are no patterns. Most—although not all—china, glass, and cooking equipment is hidden away, and accessories are either very modern or unadorned, such as the basic metal trashcan.

Stainless-steel ranges and refrigerators used to be confined to professional catering stores—and it's worth visiting these to see what's available—but electrical discount stores now stock affordable stainless-steel items for private homes. If you want a steel counter, ask your builder to cut a template and track down steelworking firms via the telephone directory or the internet—it's cheaper than going through a kitchen design company.

garden-room dining

Contemporary home extensions, with their full-length glass windows and doors and conservatory-style roofing, are designed to make the best use of light and garden views. Here is another instance in which most of the budget will probably be spent on the architecture and building, with relatively little left for furniture—as you will be aware if you are involved in a major project of this sort.

Thrift-store pieces are ideal for this kind of space because it won't matter if sunlight damages the surfaces, and contemporary plastics or garden furniture can also work well. The chairs illustrated here have been acquired in ones and twos over the years, but they look good together because they all come from the same era.

Modern furniture is well suited to this type of home extension, but you can create stunning effects by adding dramatic or elaborate pieces such as the ornate mirror shown here. The chairs are a mixture of mid-20th-century designs, including an Eames dining chair. It is worth familiarizing yourself with the works of some leading Modernist designers because originals and reproductions of these are widely available secondhand, or relatively cheap new, and are the classics of the future.

above right When choosing an antique mirror, simply pick one you love—it will work in almost any interior. But don't buy antiques under the illusion that they will always be good investments.

below right Brightly colored flowers can be used to add vibrancy to a neutral decorative scheme.

far right Gray-painted walls and dark beams make a low-key but up-to-date background for both modern and antique furniture.

glass on glass

A paneled tongue-and-groove, gray-painted room with a display of Victorian pressed glass sounds traditional, but this combination looks modern and fashionable. The secrets of success in making such displays works are simplicity and a strong linking theme. In this case, each piece of glass is different, but all the items come from the same era and are made by the same method. If you have an everyday dining table and a second table that you need only occasionally—when entertaining guests, for example—use the second table for displays. These can be quickly cleared away when necessary, and in the meantime you will have an ideal way of enjoying your collections.

left Victorian pressed glass arranged on a dining table in front of full-length windows makes a light and refreshing combination. A window display should not try to compete with the views on the other side of the glass.

right Pressed glass was developed for the manufacture of doorknobs in the 19th century, but the method was soon adapted to create cheap mass-produced glassware. Victorian and early 20th-century pressed-glass bowls, vases, cakestands, and plates have exquisite charm and can often be found at low prices in antique shops and markets.

comfortable retro

Occupying center stage in a vacation home beside the sea, the delightful room shown here and on the following pages is probably the thriftiest of all the kitchens featured in this book. It was constructed out of scaffolding boards, cinder or breeze blocks, and plaster, and furnished with hand-me-downs and bargains from secondhand sales.

Many of the furnishings are the sort of thing that people might find when clearing out their grandparents' homes. They are often dismissed as old-fashioned and of no value—but a large proportion of the mass-market furniture of the early and mid 20th century was very well designed and of sound construction. Items such as the 1960s kitchen chairs have survived for 50 years and will last for at least as long again. The homemade curtains stretched across shelves in place of doors was a popular 1950s trick—they are cheap, easy to make, and you can change them as often as you like.

right The chimney breast is shelved to use as a storage unit. To its right is an old filing cabinet, whose deep pull-out drawers are perfect for cooking pans. The 1960s kitchen chairs and enamel-topped table are typical of items that people often discard or give away.

below left A pretty homemade curtain has been hung to conceal clutter.

below center Standard white tiles make a chic backsplash and countertop.

below This sink unit was made of hollow concrete blocks and scaffolding planks and plastered over, then a tiled countertop and curtain were added. A framed vintage map of the area has been hung on the wall.

To keep renovation costs to a minimum, the owners of this vacation home decided to employ recycled building materials wherever possible. As a result, cinder or breeze blocks, and scaffolding planks were used as the basis for many of the kitchen structures. As illustrated here, the upended blocks were placed at the sides, supporting the weight of the scaffolding planks, which are used as shelving, as a base for the counter, and as seating. Both were then plastered, and striped coastal-style cushions were added to the bench, while the kitchen countertops were covered with plain white tiles.

The refrigerator housing was constructed in the same way, and sometimes a small curtain is drawn over the top part of it to conceal the microwave oven. A paneled/tongue-and-groove cupboard door has been attached to the refrigerator door with super-strength glue so that it looks like a pantry or larder rather than a standard kitchen appliance.

right White paint and blue-and-white striped cushions give the bench a nautical air. A ledge at the upper end of the paneling provides a shelf for ephemera, while a vase made out of an old vacuum flask adorns the windowsill.

below left A single shelf running along the top of the tiled area offers storage space for items in frequent use, such as teapots, salt and pepper grinders, and food-storage jars.

below Plastered cinder or breeze blocks and scaffolding planks make a frame for the refrigerator and a paneled door has been glued on to the front.

relaxed elegance

This calm, pretty dining room manages to be both elegant and casual at the same time. If you want to achieve this effect in your own home, the most important thing is to keep things simple. Another high priority is the restrained use of color.

To achieve the subtle effect that characterizes the decoration of this room, consult paint cards that show colors from their palest (with the most white added) to their darkest. The walls here are white with the barest hint of gray; the woodwork and radiator have been painted a shade darker; and the mirror slightly darker still. Apart from the big mirror, decoration has been kept to a bare minimum. It consists of no more than a few shapely green pitchers, a pair of chandeliers, and a set of characterful French chairs.

The other element worthy of mention is the chunky antique radiator. A radiator such as this is likely to be a major investment—even reconditioned ones aren't cheap— but it can make a big difference to the room.

left The combination of three shades of pale gray, a bargain table found at an antique store, and a set of comfortable old French dining chairs creates an atmosphere that is both peaceful and harmonious.

right This window overlooks the street, but privacy has been provided cheaply and easily by pinning up a single piece of voile or muslin with tiny pegs. See page 148 for making instructions. Simple pitchers such as these look good in threes.

modern open-plan

left Opening the double doors transforms the ground floor of this converted school into a large open-plan area. If your living space is open-plan, think about how the arrangement of furniture looks in the long view.

above The marble countertop was salvaged from a wet-fish stall.

above right These Verner Panton chairs are modern classics. Their wipe-down plastic surface makes them highly practical.

It is easy to find great designs from the 1950s onward at auctions and in secondhand shops, and many are perfect for open-plan living spaces. Some styles have become modern classics, such as the plastic chairs by Verner Panton. If you are buying modern furniture new, you may be worried that it will soon be out-of-date, but a mix of contemporary and traditional is a great look, and good design always fits into more than one context. Before coming to this converted school, the Panton chairs were at home in a Victorian townhouse and a country barn. The boxy chairs were bought in a chain-store sale in the 1980s and have been re-covered several times.

The dining and living areas shown above are at the other end of the open-plan living space depicted on the previous pages. Any open-plan interiors or rooms on a large scale demand large-scale furniture—if you move from an ordinary house to a loft apartment or converted warehouse, factory, or school, or even to a house with much larger rooms than you had before, some of your furniture may not look right. The good news for thrifty people is that relatively few of us want huge sofas and dining tables, so, if you are buying secondhand or at auction, big pieces will probably cost no more—and perhaps less—than their more compact counterparts.

above The simple square sofas in a basic sackcloth gray were bought in a sale at a specialist sofa store.

above left The dining table is an old school-room table and the surface is scarred and scratched from use by generations of children. Its lovely weathered patina means that the there's no need for the owners to worry about what new marks are made on it.

above Odd corners and hallways—such as this ante-hall between the kitchen and the main living space—can provide useful extra storage space.

above right This charming French armoire was originally designed for storing hats; hatpins and other accessories were kept in the lower drawer. It is now used to store china. See page 152 for advice on painting furniture.

Large furniture does cost more when bought new, however, so plan your purchasing strategy carefully. Take measurements and consider colors, then look out for chain-store sales and look up direct-mail internet companies. When choosing a large sofa, remember that simple chunky shapes and neutral shades will give you the most flexibility in the long term. You can also save money by choosing a very basic fabric covering. It is difficult to make pattern work well over a large area—and patterns date more quickly than solids colors—so you need to be sure of your judgment to get it right. Lastly, check any sofa for comfort before you buy it.

polished plaster

This warm, welcoming dining area looks as if it had had some expensive paint treatment on the walls and ceiling. In fact, the bare plaster has been sealed with a single coat of wood glue—cheaper in decorating time, and therefore labor costs, than the more usual two coats of latex or emulsion paint. However, sealing plaster may not be appropriate for houses more than 150 years old since walls from earlier times need to "breathe."

This room was created by designer and decoupage expert Lou Rota. Her signature bug-covered china and quirky "nature" mobiles can be seen on the table and at the windows. Mismatched chairs from thrift stores are combined with clean modern kitchen units from a chain store. Rota's tip for garage or car-boot sales is to take a pad of paper and a pen (it makes you look official) and not to look too interested when asking the price.

below Pitchers, plates, and cup-and-saucer sets can be found cheaply in ones and twos in charity stores and at markets.

below left Garlands are for life, not just for Christmas—festive lights look good all year round. Here, pieces of Victorian, Edwardian, and 1930s china bought at clearance sales have been updated with Rota's bug designs.

right The warmth and texture of plaster, sealed with wood glue, gives these walls depth and interest. The furniture is a mix of plain woods, and there is very little pattern or color in the decoration. This makes Rota's floral plates, pitchers, and 1930s vases look delightfully contemporary.

This kitchen is a beautiful illustration of how the basic formula of plain inexpensive chain-store units combined with a top-quality counter can produce a highly individual result. The theme here is white and steel— and it is reflected in some way in all the kitchen fixtures, equipment, countertops, and even in the cooking utensils, china, glass, and storage jars. This is a clean, calm, sophisticated look that is very simple to achieve. You can mix expensive elements with cheap chain-store lines, and you can add later discoveries as you come across them—it will all look good together. Introduce color or texture by painting the walls—as with the polished plaster walls shown here—or by hanging pictures or displaying accessories, or keep the look bright and white.

above These shelves have been covered in plasterboard and then plastered so they can be painted or treated to match the wall. There is a solid, sculptural quality to them, which makes them a good background for plain glass and white china; they would also look great with brightly colored peasant pottery.

above left Chain-store units are combined with a counter in Staron, a solid surface material made from a mix of minerals and polyester or acrylic. Similar to Corian, Staron is very hardwearing and its use is widespread in restaurants, schools, hotels, and hospitals.

above The white molded sink and simple chrome faucet or tap work as well with 1930s or Victorian china as they would with modern vases and pitchers. The molded countertop is thicker than average, which gives it a reassuringly chunky feel.

above right A full-length storage cupboard can hold a huge amount of paraphernalia, and yet, at the end of a line of units, it almost disappears into the walls, making it less obtrusive than cabinets above the counter. The extractor hood, range, refrigerator, and trashcan all have a similar metallic look.

A line of cabinets along one wall, with an L-shape of units on the other side of the room, all beneath the counter, offers a large area for food preparation, with open shelves, racks, and rods above to keep the atmosphere light and airy. A full-length cupboard at the end of one run of units offers plenty of storage space. There is no attempt to disguise equipment—a big stainless-steel refrigerator and stove add a modern feel to the room, and the row of stainless-steel cooking utensils hanging behind the stove is practical as well as attractive. The chunky shelves and thicker-than-average counter add an unusual textural quality. The shelves were bought at a chain store, covered in plasterboard, plastered, and, like the walls, sealed with wood glue.

pure and simple

In this kitchen, the ceiling, walls, cabinets, and stove are all white, removing the need to disguise white appliances or to worry about what goes with what. An all-white scheme makes spaces seem larger. You could achieve the same effect with cream, gray, or any neutral color, but the advantage of choosing white as the background color is that most kitchen fixtures, including sinks, dishwashers, refrigerators, and countertops, are cheaply available as white basics, so will seamlessly fit in with their surroundings. The approach works well in rooms with quirky shapes or period features.

right This rustic table was discovered in an antique shop in France—even though you may have to pay shipping costs, you can still find bargains abroad.

below Choosing white for the ceiling, walls, cabinets, cooking range, dishwasher, sink, and counter opens up the space and offsets the effect of a low ceiling. An all-white scheme also looks fresh, clean, and modern while preserving the character of this period home.

Many everyday objects have an intrinsic beauty, so don't hide them away. Wooden spoons, storage jars, pestles and mortars, and other kitchen utensils are much more useful when they are close at hand, and putting them on show doesn't have to make the room look cluttered. In a kitchen where you have decided to keep down spending on kitchen units, simply displaying utilitarian items in containers has a decorative effect.

Recycling packaging for your own use is good for your pocket and good for the environment. Instead of sending empty glass jars to a landfill site, you can either reuse them for homemade jams and jellies, give them to friends who make preserves, or use them for storing all sorts of other things—anything from loose change to foodstuffs such as beans, nuts, and pasta. With their lids off, they will hold kitchen utensils, and smaller jars can be used as holders for votive candles.

left Glass candle-holders, a pestle and mortar, and a tile from Taormina in Sicily make a composition that is both pretty and practical. Odd tiles can be picked up very cheaply and are useful if you need to put down something hot on a kitchen counter.

below left These delightful jam jars have been decorated with buttons by stylist Sania Pell. They make great containers for a collection of wooden spoons and spatulas, chopsticks and wooden barbecue skewers. See page 149 for making instructions.

below Wooden chopping boards and bread boards are stacked ready for use. Every kitchen needs at least four chopping boards: one for raw meat, one for cooked meat, one for vegetables, and one for bread. If you buy boards of different sizes and shapes, you can keep track of what is used for what.

living spaces

Thrifty style can work across a wide range of styles: classic, contemporary, retro, country, modern, and eclectic. You can get big ticket items, such as sofas and chairs, in sales or auctions, concentrating on simple shapes and neutral colors. Then fabrics, art, lighting, and flooring can be collected or adapted as you go along. An empty living space often looks smarter than one that is over-crowded, so if you can't afford exactly what you want, leave a space for it later.

contemporary classic

Thrifty chic does not have to mean bohemian or scruffy. This contemporary living room is elegant and stylish, a happy mix of modern and classic pieces. Sofas and armchairs are the big-ticket items in living spaces, but you can reduce costs by buying at sales or secondhand. Go for simple shapes in solid, neutral colors. Secondhand sofas are always cheap, but having an old sofa reupholstered could cost half as much as buying a new one. It's only worth it in the case of a traditionally made sprung sofa—if yours is a modern foam version, have new slipcovers made or use throws and pillows to ring the changes.

left In this room painted in soft, neutral paint colors, classic furniture is mixed with modern pieces. The Sputnik light is an original designer piece, but cheap chain-store reproductions can be found. The coffee table, a Charles Eames design, was bought secondhand.

right The yellow sofa was a hand-me-down and the leather chair is one of a pair from a thrift store. They have been updated with geometrically patterned pillows, a plain Swedish linen window shade, a contemporary print, and a stylish black lamp.

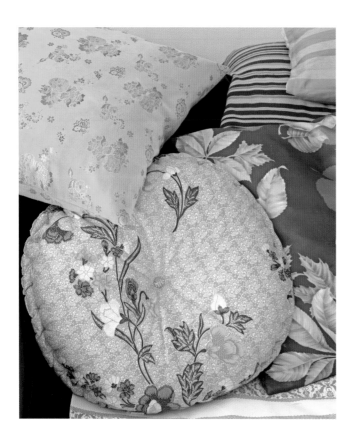 

These pages illustrate how you can give an old sofa a lively contemporary edge by adorning it with pillows and throws. Mixing color and pattern in this way is a thrifty way to decorate because you can use a small amount of expensive fabric in combination with cheaper materials. You may also be able to re-use hand-me-down fabrics, old blankets, pieces of clothing, or second-hand curtains, by turning them into pillow covers.

This is an approach that has long been seen as the secret to achieving the faded country-house look, but you can sharpen it up for contemporary urban living by using a controlled color palette, such as the red/orange/pink/purple spectrum shown here, and keeping all the other elements in the room low-key and subdued. The walls, shutters, and even the lamp are in similar neutral tones, and any other elements, such as the flowers and the retro glass ashtray, reflect the pink and red theme.

above left Combining pillows in two different stripes and three types of floral fabric could look old-fashioned, but in this case their zany, punchy colors and unfussy shapes make a high-fashion impact.

above You can buy remnants of high-end designer fabrics at bargain prices on the internet. Interior design stores usually have bins full of ends of rolls at a big discount, too.

right Give an old sofa a new lease on life with contemporary pillows and a throw. For modern design and retro chic, pick up inexpensive glass ashtrays from thrift stores and use them for serving olives or peanuts.

an eclectic mix

Most items shown on these pages have been sewn, knitted, crocheted, or stitched by hand—evidence that craft and needlework are reasserting their influence among today's cost-conscious consumers. The lampshade, throw, pillows, and crocheted blanket were all homemade, and all the furniture came from auctions, thrift stores, and local sales. Many large towns have a "general auction," which is a great place to find secondhand home furnishings. When visiting an antique market, find out when it starts and arrive as early as possible. At the end of the day, there won't be much left, but a dealer may give you a good reduction to save having to pack up something and take it home.

left The throw is a pretty fabric remnant in a light cotton that could easily get crumpled and rucked up, but it has been given shape and "weighted down" by being attached on the underside to an old wool blanket. The two pillows started their useful life as grain sacks and the lampshade is homemade.

right The armchair and two side tables were all bought at an auction. Check carefully for damage before bidding— repairs can be expensive.

books, books, books

Book-lovers can sometimes be overwhelmed by the challenge of storing the objects of their passion. A single bookcase is never enough, and even a whole wall of shelves can start to overflow. If you are building bookshelves, there are a few tips worth remembering—for example, shorter shelves won't bow in the middle. Many people prefer to reduce the height of the shelves nearer the ceiling to stop the bookshelf looking as if it were toppling forward. You can take the height up to the ceiling or, in higher-ceilinged rooms, stop at picture-rail level.

We have recently started to recognize the potential of books as design objects. Some book covers, especially those from the days when cover art was starting to emerge as a fashion, are examples of great design and deliciously evocative of their age. Thrift stores, secondhand bookstores, and the internet are all good sources of vintage volumes.

left These books are arranged by color—which not only looks attractive but, for those who can't always remember the name of an author, is also a surprisingly effective way of finding the title you want. If you like to have woodwork the same tone as your walls, or even a degree or two darker, for dramatic effect chose a slightly darker shade again for the bookshelves.

right Make the most of eye-catching covers by turning books face out. Vintage covers are a hot new area for collectors. Even in genres that have not traditionally been seen as "serious"—such as Westerns or romantic fiction—the covers were often commissioned from highly talented artists and designers.

paint harmony

The most economical way to decorate any room, to update thrift-store finds, or make chain-store purchases look more expensive is to use paint. This vacation home on the south coast of England has been given a light, airy feel with a subtle palette of white and gray, softened by a pretty chandelier and delightful French chairs. To achieve a similar harmonious effect, consult paint cards with graduated shades of the same color. In the room illustrated, the walls are off-white, the woodwork is a shade deeper, and the mirror and console table are slightly darker again. The chosen color spectrum ranges from off-white through gray to olive green, echoing the gray-green sea outside the window.

Exposed historic brickwork and lime mortar can look great, but harsh modern bricks with cement mortar are less attractive. If you have bare brick that you don't like and can't afford to plaster, simply paint it directly.

right The console table is a chain-store model painted a chic gray. Like most elements of this seaside home, it was a thrifty purchase, but the owner has splurged on one or two items. In this room, a couple of reconditioned antique radiators were the big indulgence— but they really enhance the atmosphere.

below left The sofa came from an internet direct-sale company and the pillows were made up from fabric scraps bought at garage or car-boot sales.

below You can find little chests such as this in almost any thrift store. Apart from being given a practical new slate top, this one has been left untouched.

sale bargains

Consisting of two large interlinked rooms that were once part of an old schoolhouse, this fashionable interior was put together by combining items from store sales, pillows made from leftover scraps of fabric, and a mixture of modern art and children's paintings on the walls. Big rooms look best with large-scale furniture, so this is where most of the budget has been spent. Two matching modern sofas—with clean lines, in the simplest and plainest fabric option—were bought at a sofa workshop sale, and the rest of the room took shape around them.

When buying furniture at store sales, use the same approach as when buying clothes. Spend time window-shopping to get an idea of what you want, and make sure the piece you're interested in is really right for you. In the case of big-ticket items such as sofas, avoid extremes of fashion and make sure they are comfortable and the measurements are correct.

above left The neutral gray sofas work with almost any color or style. The pillow on the right was made from a remnant of curtain fabric, while the one on the left was stitched by the house's owner.

above center Although this former school building dates from the Victorian era, the fact that it is a conversion means that, in this setting, modern furniture looks as good as—or even better than—traditional items.

above This combination of modern art and framed children's paintings is very successful. Frame the children's work with as much care as you would the real artists' pieces.

right The plastic bucket chair is a modern design classic, which would be as useful outside in the garden as when paired with elegant furniture in the living room.

faded grandeur

There is more than a suggestion of the historic home about this rural cottage in southern England. It was built about a hundred years ago, to relatively modest specifications, but such is the exuberance of its style that it feels like a large bohemian country house. The compact and comfortable leather armchairs resemble old family friends, while the double doors were rescued from a dumpster/skip and reglazed. The blue-and-white-striped curtains with their bobble fringes, and the way in which they swirl on to the floor, add a touch of luxury, reinforcing the bold effect of the traditional English chintzes on the armchair.

left Small armchairs are worth snapping up because, however faded and battered, they are often far more comfortable than bigger chairs. Bobble fringing can be bought from craft suppliers or department stores.

below left The double doors to the garden came from another house of similar vintage whose owner had discarded them.

below English country chintzes are always both welcoming and grand. If you like this look, use it on chairs, rather than sofas—it will be much cheaper and less dominating.

white rooms

White is a classic but eternally modern element of interiors—particularly in living rooms, where it provides an excellent backdrop for pictures and objets d'art. Pure white first became fashionable as a decorating color in the 1950s through the influence of the British decorator Syrie Maugham, and for about 20 years white living rooms outnumbered those in any other color. Now "historic" hues have taken over, and there are dozens of different shades of white to choose from—but sometimes a sharp, crisp "white" white is the easiest, cheapest way of making a room look clean and contemporary. If you make a full commitment to it—white walls, white ceiling, white paintwork, and white floors—you can go in any direction you like from there. Here, the look could be called modern eclectic, with boxy sofas, black-and-white photographs, and one or two older pieces.

left Both these items of furniture have been re-covered. A pale gray fabric was chosen for the boxy 1990s sofa and the cheapest, plainest upholstery fabric available for the early 19th-century chair. The simplicity of the fabrics does nothing to detract from the fine lines of both new and old pieces.

below left The gray, blue, brown, and white pebbles echo the colors of the decorative scheme that prevails in this house.

below One person's rubbish is another's lucky find. An old map chest was rescued from a dumpster/skip and is now used to store photographs, pictures, and memorabilia.

left and above This arrangement shows that traditionally crafted items can look surprisingly modern in a white room. The hand-made log baskets are works of art in themselves and should not be hidden from view.

above center The juxtaposition of a thrift-store table and a modern tripod lamp show how easy it is to combine old and new. The striking floral vase looks particularly dramatic against an all-white wall.

above right This "blanket" pillow came from a store specializing in British country crafts. If you have lovely old blankets that are worn or torn, you could consider cutting them up to make pillow covers in this way.

White is particularly effective in period homes because the high ceilings and large windows in many such homes offer the space and light that allow the white to come into its own, while the period detailing helps to prevent a bland result. Modern white radiators can merge visually with the wall color, and uneven ceilings or low beams can also be made less prominent without losing them altogether. White on white or pale neutrals on white create a light, Scandinavian feel, but the combination of dark wood, leather, and fabric against a white wall is also striking. Naturally textured materials such as wicker, linen, and wool show up well against a white background.

If your décor is looking tired and faded but you have very little money, buy a pot of paint and spend a weekend painting everything white. It's the quickest and cheapest total transformation available, and your entire living spaces will suddenly feel bright, clean, and new.

above Necklaces and ribbons should not be hidden away because they can add sparkle and color to a simple decorative scheme.

right The pillows on this sofa incorporate a mixture of fabrics and textures. There has been no attempt to match them to each other or to other furnishings in the room. If you adopt this relaxed approach, you can pick up beautiful pillows in ones and twos when you spot them.

treasures on display

You don't need expensive collections to create an attractive display, but you do need to think carefully about how you arrange objects. One technique is to "crowd it up"—a well-tried antique dealer's trick—and another, illustrated here, is to give everything plenty of space. The color in this room comes from children's artwork, propped up alongside ordinary glasses and candle-holders. The important thing is not how much items cost but whether you like the combination of colors and shapes—and some of the humblest everyday objects can look beautiful. Even pretty necklaces and ribbons can be part of the decoration. If you keep your displays sparkling clean, they will have more impact; and items that are used regularly are much less likely to gather dust.

The sofa is piled with pillows in different colors and textures, which gives a much more relaxed, modern feel than it would have if all the elements were carefully matched. You can pick up eye-catching pillows at store sales or buy small pieces of designer fabrics on the internet. If you visit Ebay, for example, and put your favorite fabric company's name into the "search" field, you will be given plenty of choice, but it is not always particularly easy to see what you are getting, and the fabric quantities offered for sale are rarely large enough for curtains or other big projects.

bedrooms and bathrooms

Bedrooms and bathrooms are today's ultimate sanctuaries but, as this chapter shows, they do not have to cost the earth. Visit store sales to find high-quality new beds and bedlinen at affordable prices, but everything else for the bedroom can be bought at secondhand stores or in auctions. And while it's never wise to economize on plumbing, the most basic bathroom fixtures can be made to look luxurious with the right accessories.

when less really is more

It may sound odd to say so, but one of the cheapest decorating tricks is to do nothing—or, at least, to do the absolute minimum. Many of us feel under pressure to make our homes a reflection of our personal style, so it's worth remembering that we are not obliged to redecorate a room unless it's ugly or really shabby. The contrasting "ice cream" colors in the two bedrooms illustrated on these pages were chosen by the previous inhabitants of the house, and its new owners then spent a weekend scouring local thrift stores to furnish it. If you decide on a unifying theme rather than trying to make everything match—here, it is a mix of soft pinks, blues, and apricot—you can buy one thing at a time rather than getting everything all at once.

The biggest investment in a bedroom is the bed, and no one likes secondhand mattresses. However, you can buy vintage or secondhand beds and pair them with new mattresses. The bed frames in these rooms came from an antique store specializing in iron bedsteads.

below left Small tables like this one can be bought cheaply in antique stores everywhere. There is no need for tables on each side of the bed to match.

below Bedlinen collected over the years can be mixed with ordinary white cotton sheets, perhaps adding in a few expensive pillowslips.

right These antique bed frames have been given new mattresses. It is often unnecessary to restore or respray old frames since a few blemishes give an authentic retro feel.

Simplicity always works well in bedrooms. After all, it was not until the early part of the 20th century that an average bedroom would have contained more than a bed, a chamber pot (perhaps in its pot cabinet), a few pegs on the wall or in a small cupboard, and somewhere to put a candle. Many people had only one set of clothes for daily wear and something more elegant for Sundays, which they hung on hooks. The delightful seaside bedroom shown opposite harks back to those more peaceful days before armoires and built-in closets became an indispensable part of the home.

There is now an increasing trend toward making bedrooms simpler again, but because so many of us have large quantities of clothes and possessions, we cannot do without storage. If you have any free space in your bathroom, line it with cupboards for clothes—or, if your landing is wide enough, there may be room to install useful closets there. A bedroom with a walk-in closet—or what would have been called a dressing-room in an earlier age—is a particular luxury, while some of us reduce the need for home storage by having our winter or summer clothes professionally stored when they are not being worn. Other people keep out-of-season clothes in boxes or suitcases under the bed.

The problem of storage throws light on the whole philosophy of thrift. Frugal homeowners aim to minimize all kinds of possessions, and a growing number·of people believe in buying new clothes only when the old ones wear out. If you could follow this model, you too could have a bedroom with just a row of pegs along the wall. Most of us couldn't live like this, but it's not impossible, and a room like the one shown here stands to remind us of what we could do. Perhaps the main challenge offered by this room is to question whether we need to have as much as we do—and if we would sleep better and feel happier with fewer possessions around us.

right Some experts believe that the key to a good night's sleep is to have a bedroom that is simple, uncluttered, and free of all electrical items, such as televisions, digital radios, and alarm clocks. When you are on vacation, all you need in your sleeping space are plain paneled walls, old iron beds, mix-and-match sheets, a single mirror, and a row of pegs.

an attic retreat

Attic rooms are quirky spaces that frequently suffer from a lack of light, so when it comes to decorating an attic, there are two options—to make the most of what light there is and paint the room in pale colors, or to use deep or rich colors on the walls for a cozy effect. If you choose the pale route, brighten it up with a rich or strong bedcover, a dramatic painting, or something colorful to prevent the room from looking drab. If you use the same color all over, without trying to distinguish the ceiling from the walls, it will look more spacious.

Low-rise furniture works well in attics, even in those rooms where the head height is not too restricted, as the relative proportions create a more pleasing effect. The bed shown here has a headboard made from a piece of thick ply or MDF cut to size, padded with white wadding, then wrapped in fabric and stapled together. You can buy similar headboards for five times the cost of this homemade version. For a larger room, you could scale it up—indeed, this one used to be in an ordinary room and had to be cut down to size to fit in this attic retreat.

left Bought 15 years ago at a trendy home store, the contemporary-looking light offers another example of the timelessness of good modern design. Red is a great color for perking up an attic, and this rich red Scandinavian blanket and spotted pillow are good mood-lifters.

right This haven of a bedroom is in the roof of a converted school. A low bed with a homemade headboard (see page 144) costs a fraction of its designer counterparts.

vintage modern

One of the great interior design trends of the decade is to combine ultramodern with battered vintage items. Vintage furniture adds soul to a modern interior, while the crisp clean lines of modern lighting, for example, give vintage furniture a new edge. This is a look that makes a house into a home rather than a pale imitation of a furniture catalog, and it is very affordable. A huge selection of modern lighting is now available from chain stores, where you can also find simple, good-quality designs in china, bedding, and furniture.

Like the headboard, the bedside cabinets shown here are French, but similar small chests can be seen in thrift stores everywhere. It is difficult to find two that match—and pairs usually fetch a premium price—but you should be able to find two of about the same size, shape, and color. "Pot cupboards" are bedroom chests made to hold chamber pots in the days, not so long ago, when plumbing was basic, and there are still plenty of them available in antique stores.

left A charming French headboard has been paired with a French pot cupboard, which serves as a bedside table. Modern lighting and crisp cotton sheets make a stylish contrast to the distressed painted wood—when buying battered furniture, you don't necessarily have to paint it since the patina of age often has more character than new paint.

right A second pot cupboard on the other side of the same bed shows that there is no need for bedside tables to match exactly.

bedroom neutrals

above and top Just a few blooms in a little vase can transform a room. Florists often sell flowers by the stem—for a chic look, display them on their own in separate vases, rather than putting them all together in one big vase.

above right Texture is the main story here: crisp white sheets, basic upholstery linen, carved wood, and a modern steel lamp make a harmonious combination.

The light-filled, understated bedrooms illustrated on these pages suggest an atmosphere of peace and tranquility. This is achieved by combining a scheme of pale neutrals—shades of bone, white, cream, and gray—with the textures of natural materials such as linen, wood, and stone. There is a minimal use of pattern or color. It is a look that is both fashionable and classic and is particularly soothing in bedrooms. For a splash of uplifting color, add a posy of flowers or some richly hued pillows and throws.

above A thrift-store chest of drawers and mirror painted to match are offset by some brightly colored flowers in a stoneware vase.

above right Furniture painted white, cream, and bone, and a chair upholstered in gray linen create a calm corner. The curtains are made of old French linen sheets and the lampshade is also homemade.

"Neutrals and naturals" is an easy look to put together but, in the absence of pattern, it relies for interest on contrasting textures. Consider the effects that can be achieved by juxtaposing painted wood with polished wood, a linen weave with a smoothly painted wall, and soft wool with a collection of hard, shiny china and glass objects. All these elements are available at every price level—some of the cheapest furnishing fabrics to be found are the very basic plain linens, cottons, and weaves.

mixing pattern

Inexpensive fabrics often come in harsh colors or unattractive patterns, and they may look just a little too bright or shiny, so it's a challenge to make them appear chic. These fabrics here all come from top-quality designer brands, but a small quantity has been made to go a long way. Headboards and stools usually require just a few short lengths of fabric, which you can often find as remnants, off-cuts, or leftovers in fabric or interior design stores. Internet auction sites are also a good source of short runs of designer fabric, although it is quite hard to tell exact shades or colors from online photographs.

right A mix of wonderful designer fabrics are shown here, but each item only uses a small amount of fabric. Pick a tone or theme: here the soft lilac shade anchors the scheme,contrasted with primrose yellow. Although there are several different patterns—toiles, checks, and a large paisley—the whole story is about lilac contrasted with yellow or cream, making it harmonious and not too fussy.

left Recycle your fabrics: this bedspread is made from an old curtain, edged with a yellow linen that picks up the yellow in the floral pattern. To give it weight, it has been backed with wadding and lined.

modern romantic

In the same way that roses are the flowers of romance, pink is its color, but pink is often disregarded because of its association with fairytales and plastic toys. Pink adds both warmth and light to a room, however, and psychological tests have repeatedly shown that it has a very calming and soothing effect. It is an ideal color for bedlinen, and you can avoid cliché by introducing it in a clean, bright, modern context. The bed shown here is adorned by recently purchased new bedlinen and a secondhand quilt—which is not only thrifty but also enhances the character of the room.

Recycling vintage fabric—whether you've inherited it, had it for some time, or bought it secondhand—can introduce an interesting new element to a bedroom that's otherwise furnished in familiar fashionable patterns. Combine new bedlinen—a delicious pair of pillowslips you've found in a sale, a "seconds" cotton sheet with a high thread-count, or an extravagant new duvet cover, for example—with vintage cottons, linens, and quilts, and refresh the appearance of sheets and covers that you've had for a long time.

Old curtains can be recycled as bedcovers, as can bin-ends of fabric that you might not otherwise have been able to afford. If your bedroom is decorated in calm, plain neutrals such as white, gray, or cream, the effect will be pretty but contemporary.

above New floral and striped bedlinen paired with a secondhand vintage quilt make an enticing combination.

left Set against white walls, furniture and lamp, and a simple headboard, also in white, this group of pink prints looks fresh and contemporary. The fairy lights above the bedhead add extra sparkle.

fresh and colorful

Decorating a bathroom offers a good opportunity for indulging in a touch of fantasy or using lively colors that might look out of place elsewhere. The examples seen on these pages include a bathroom that reminds its users of the countryside and the sea—even if the views outside are of city streets—and one where a few vivid accessories make you feel cheerful, even on the darkest days.

The country-feel bathroom incorporates a standard bathtub, made to look more distinctive by the addition of a traditional Victorian-style faucet or tap, and surrounded with tongue-and-groove wood paneling instead of tiling. Ready-made paneling is available cheaply from handyman/DIY

above left Wood paneling is a cheap but classic alternative to tiling. If you are worried about water damage in a bathroom, protect the wood with exterior-use paint.

above A standard basin and toilet are given a lift by towels in bright, fashionable colors.

above A collection of vibrantly colored hot-water bottles is amusing and welcoming.

above right This flamboyant lampshade came from one of the country craft fairs that tour Britain in summer. Such fairs are good sources of unusual or handmade items.

stores. Wood stands up well to bathroom use—but, if you want a higher level of water resistance, you can always decorate it with exterior paint.

The white bathroom with its vibrant towels and accessories—including the gaily colored hot-water bottles and "bath-hat" lampshade—shows how a small, ordinary room with no expensive treatments can still look enticing. It includes an old-fashioned, stand-alone towel rail of a type that can still be found in chain stores, hung with towels in fashionably bright colors. Thick white towels, like white bedlinen, have long been a symbol of luxury—but the growing popularity of pattern and color signals a refreshing change.

statement wallpaper

This bedroom with connecting bathroom exemplifies an ultramodern use of wallpaper—a dramatic pattern as the main decorative element, teamed with simple curtains, paintwork, and accessories. Wallpaper is making a comeback, and although it is not cheap, using it in this way means that you can splash out on the paper and economize on other elements, such as the curtains. There no need to have coordinating wallpaper and fabric—indeed, it is more fashionable not to. Using wallpaper on a single wall will reduce the cost, as will picking up bargains at sales.

left A striking wallpaper enlivens an otherwise understated room, in which the colors and fabrics are low-key and the bedside lamps are small and discreet. Installing paneled closets and headboard has overcome the problem of the bed being wider than the chimney breast.

right Modern accessories—a wicker chair, popular in the 1960s and 1970s, and a contemporary photo frame—make it clear that this is wallpaper 21st-century style. To offset the busy pattern, the photo frame is very simple, with black-and-white pictures.

Thrifty bathrooms are tricky. Buying secondhand sanitaryware—bathtubs, washbasins, toilets, and faucets or taps—is generally unsatisfactory, and it is rare to see a lovely vintage sink in an antique store. However, architectural salvage yards are good sources of rescued cast-iron bathtubs. Condition is all-important—a cracked sink or a stained bathtub is not pleasant to use and could even put people off buying your house if you are trying to sell. Tubs can be resurfaced, at a cost. If you are buying a vintage bathtub, check that the supplier has provided proper conversion connections. You don't want to spend a fortune on reconditioning a tub only to discover that it is incompatible with modern plumbing installations.

The best way of saving money in a bathroom is to spend most of your budget on one outstanding item—the bathtub, say—and resort to plumbers' basics for the rest.

right A traditional clawfoot bathtub is the big-ticket item in this bathroom; everything else is kept simple. There is no wooden surround or tiling—just elegant gray paint and a thrift-store table to hold bathroom essentials.

below left This integrated sink was cut from a piece of Corian; interior designer Clare Nash drew a plan for the manufacturers to follow. It is slotted into an MDF console table built by a carpenter and painted light gray.

below The unusual towel rail was made from a length of acrylic, cut to the right size, and then attached by ordinary chrome towel-rail holders. The faucets, or taps, are a clever mixture of traditional and modern elements.

retro bathrooms

Most of the elements of the bathroom illustrated on these pages have been sourced from architectural salvage yards at relatively low cost. Architectural salvage has become very fashionable in recent years, and a lot of salvage yards charge what can seem like quite high prices, but there are always bargains to be had for sharp-eyed customers, and this cast-iron rolltop bath—bought through a website that brings together buyers and sellers of antique, reclaimed, salvaged, and green items—is just one of them.

Tiling is one area of the decorative scheme in your bathroom where it is possible to save money. Many contemporary bathrooms are tiled from floor to ceiling—but this is not necessary, unless you like the look. A well-designed, well-ventilated room painted in a specially formulated bathroom paint is unlikely to suffer significant problems from damp. Make sure there are no little areas where water can be trapped, and repair leaks in faucets or pipes whenever they appear. While you are using the bathroom, keep a lookout for areas that could become damp. Vigilance is as effective as wall-to-ceiling tiling—if not more so.

left A rolltop bath from an architectural salvage yard is set against a background of painted paneled tongue-and-groove walls. If you decide not to tile your bathroom, make sure there are no corners where water can lie undetected—or you may suffer problems from damp.

top right This toilet tank looks old but it is, in fact, modern. However, the china knob at the end of the chain is a genuine antique.

center right A salvaged sink and piece of opaline glass are backed by ordinary white tiles, which have been arranged to resemble bricks for an appropriately retro feel.

below right Marble-topped tables are perfect for bathrooms and can be found in abundance at auctions and thrift stores. Pretty candles add atmosphere—but remember never to leave a burning candle unattended.

Both the bathtub and the sink illustrated on these pages were bought through a plumbers' catalog and were very reasonably priced. The tub is an acrylic reproduction that has been made to look chic by the addition of a coat of dark gray paint. A cheap wooden towel rail has been painted the same shade of gray as the walls. It is really worth getting to know what fixtures are on the market, then seeing what you can buy cheaply at your local plumbers' merchant. Sometimes plumbers' merchants will offer you a deal—particularly if you are remodeling more than one bathroom at once.

left People sometimes hesitate to hang real pictures in bathrooms, but provided they are properly framed and not in the direct line of water, they will be fine.

right The handsome "vintage" basin was bought cheaply through a plumbers' catalog. The storage unit is a secondhand oak piece that started life in a store—the doors lift up and slide in above the shelves.

all in the detail

One way of making an inexpensive bathroom look special is to choose simple plumbers' basics for the bathtub, sink, and toilet, and make them look interesting and contemporary by adding stylish faucets or unusual accessories. In this room, standard sanitary-ware and simple white tiles have been teamed with utilitarian faucets, or taps, creating a chic, modern look and offering a neutral background for any kind of decorative treatment. The theme here could be described as "found on your travels," since the inset soap dish was salvaged from an Indian temple and the hanging pebble was picked up on a beach.

If you hide pipes behind a false wall, you can use the extra depth to create extra storage or a decorative alcove. As the photograph on the right shows, a strip of space between the tub and the window accommodates a narrow, floor-to-ceiling concealed closet. It has been given the same decorative treatment as the walls, so you can only see it's there by looking at the baseboard—there's a break where the closet door is.

Efficient planning is at the heart of any beautiful bathroom. Above all, the practical elements must work efficiently. Take careful measurements of your room, then experiment with various options. In a restricted space, you could consider installing any of the following: a big bathtub with a

top left This hanging pebble was found on a beach, complete with a convenient hole created by the action of the sea.

center left This intriguing piece of architectural salvage, which came from an Indian temple, makes an ideal holder for soap and other bathing accessories.

left Understated modern faucets, or taps, make standard white tiles look chic and contemporary.

right Extra storage has been installed in this bathroom in the form of a concealed floor-to-ceiling closet between the edge of the bath and the window.

compact sink and toilet; a large shower and no tub; a corner sink, a corner tub, and a shower—and a myriad other combinations. Wet rooms make good use of space, but avoid installing them on upper floors because they often develop leaks. Wall-hung basins, bidets, and toilets make the floor space look larger and the floor easier to clean, and storage can be wall-hung, too. Using existing pipes will save money, but you may save space by moving a sink or a tub. Putting a bathroom in a part of your home where there are no existing pipes is likely to prove very costly.

When taking measurements, bear in mind the likely physical variations of the people who will be using the bathroom. Will someone very tall or a small child be able to use the sink easily? Will left-handed people be able to brush their teeth or shave as comfortably as right-handed people? The sink illustrated here is about one foot away from the wall, so it can be used by right- or left-handed people, but if it had been an inch or so farther to the left, it would have been awkward for a left-handed person. Even toilets need elbow space, and mirror heights are critical, too.

left This sink has been sited far enough away from the wall to enable a left-handed person to use it comfortably—don't forget that the practical aspects of a bathroom are as important as how it looks.

right A pane of smooth sandblasted glass is very effective in a small bathroom. It looks contemporary and will protect your privacy, allowing you to do without curtains or shades.

gardens and outdoor spaces

Thriftiness is in the gardener's nature. Anyone who enjoys growing things loves to give, receive, or exchange plants, but pots can be expensive. You can adapt all kinds of artifacts—from sinks and troughs to vintage baby carriages and old cans—to use as planters. Even the humble garden shed can save you money. Rather than move home or build an extension, why not convert your wooden storage shed into a laundry room or office?

a shady retreat

The big expense in an outdoor space is the hard landscaping—laying terraces and paths or building fences, pergolas, and benches—while pots and plants can be collected over time. You can sink a brick or stone path into the ground yourself, but take care as it ages—the worn tips of stone flags or bricks can be tripping hazards. Gravel is easier to lay and most garden centers sell it by the bag. If you can't afford a conservatory or summer house, a simple pergola offers a charming alternative.

right A delightful pergola outside the kitchen window offers shade on a hot day and filters the sunlight for a collection of pots below. The restrained use of color is particularly chic—the white parasol and wall with the cream canvas sunbeds add up to a very stylish haven.

below left These weathered planters in a variety of shapes, sizes, and colors are the basis of a small kitchen garden. Herbs, salad vegetables, beans, tomatoes, and chilies can all be grown productively in this small space.

below You can collect pots from anywhere. Mix supermarket finds with the occasional expensive stoneware urn or even a souvenir of holidays abroad, such the Moroccan pot on the left. Large tins, sinks, and troughs can also be converted to use as pots.

left This beguiling garden seat was made by a carpenter to its owner's specifications, roofed with slate to protect it from bad weather, and painted in historic paint suitable for exterior use.

below left This little café chair is a classic design and can be used indoors and out.

below Garden chairs can be collected over time. A single chair is often much cheaper than one of a set of four or six—and there's no need for your chairs to match. Choose a theme such as teak or wirework, then assemble variations on the theme.

below center A miscellaneous collection of wirework, wicker, and terracotta, together with a small thrift-store table, gives a romantic feel to a corner of a terrace.

below right A 25-year-old wirework table looks just as modern as it did when it was new. Classic garden furniture will survive for many years, and only becomes more attractive as it weathers.

Most garden furniture is relatively inexpensive. However, mass-market white or green plastic tables and chairs not only cost little but also give an impression of cheapness. Old metalwork and weathered teak present a much more romantic image. The chairs shown on these pages are genuinely old, but you can find attractive wirework and metal furniture through auction sites on the internet or buy it quite cheaply in antique stores. A little rust is fine, but if necessary, protect people's clothing by adding pillows. Choosing garden furniture that can also be used indoors is a good idea if you like to entertain but don't have space to store lots of extra chairs.

Factory outlets are a good source of discount teak or wood furniture, or you can even construct your own garden seat from ply, MDF or pine. The beautiful covered seat shown on the opposite page was made to the owner's own design, and roofed with slate to protect it from rain damage and enable it to be used in all weathers. Leading paint companies produce a wonderful choice of historic shades for exterior use.

balconies and terraces

Adding a balcony or terrace to your home is a much cheaper option than building an extension or a conservatory, and can offer just as much extra living space—although how often you use it will depend on the weather. Check planning regulations before starting, especially in a conservation area or if you are dealing with an architecturally protected building.

A balcony lets you take advantage of any views from the upper levels of a house, makes a lovely place to have a quiet drink as the sun goes down, and also shelters the area beneath it, creating a shaded spot that can be used all summer, even when it rains. In the house illustrated here, the decking has been made from driftwood—planks that have washed up on the beach—and the furniture has been collected over many years.

right Below the balcony is a sheltered corner for an old sofa and a dining table—a useful extension of the living area in summer.

below left A collection of vintage flags and bunting adds a festive air to this balcony. You can find vintage flags in military memorabilia stores and on the internet.

below While softwood furniture should not really be left outside for any length of time, a cheap pine table painted with a good exterior paint will survive all but the wettest summers.

A garden shed can be much more than simply a place to store garden tools. In particular, it offers a way to increase your living space without having to extend your existing home or move elsewhere. The delightful sheds shown on these pages include an artist's studio-cum-library, an office, and a laundry room. It may be possible to build a shed in a place where it is not possible to build a brick building, and if it is insulated and equipped with electricity, you can work in it. Your local planning authority will tell you if you need planning permission to build a shed, but often you don't. And such a structure costs much less than an extension or attic conversion.

For the most part, these sheds were built by their owners using as many reclaimed elements as possible. All the pillars are made from fiberglass, and came from a stage set long ago, while the doors and windows were supplied by an architectural salvage company. Some materials came from elsewhere in the house. Don't forget that reclamation starts at home—save old shelving or cabinet doors or offer them to someone else who might have a use for them.

The smallest shed here houses the washing machine and dryer, freeing up essential space in the very small kitchen of the cottage it serves. It is crucial to make sure that such a structure is weatherproof —that is, protected by a proper roof and exterior-use paint—because the combination of rain and electricity could be a fatal one.

above left An "office" shed was built from reclaimed doors and windows and two fiberglass pillars from a stage set. It is fully insulated.

left Two pretty doors rescued from a coal-storage shed form the basis of this outdoor laundry room. It is painted pale green, using a hard-wearing exterior paint.

right Nicknamed "the Acropolis," this library-cum-artist's studio was built around the fiberglass pillars that its owners had had for some time and had previously used inside. The reuse of wood, shelving, and other building materials was at the heart of the project.

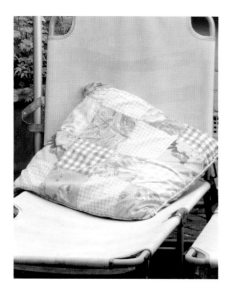

*When making a project, follow either the imperial or
the metric measurements, but do not interchange
them, since the equivalents are only approximate.*

the projects

This selection of easy-to-make projects shows how to bring
a new lease of life to existing furniture and how to add stylish,
individual touches to your home without spending a fortune.

patchwork pillow

Patchwork says "thrifty chic" more than virtually any other technique, since it traditionally incorporates scraps of fabric that cost nothing. Stitched together, they make a colorful cover for an old pillow, and the square patches mean the stitching can be quickly done on a sewing machine. If your pillow is a different size, you can use the same technique, simply adjusting the size or number of patches. Choose a selection of fabrics that are not too worn and that are the same thickness, weight, and type of fiber (cotton is ideal). Piping made from one of the fabrics has been used around the edges to add definition, but you could use readymade bias binding instead—or not pipe the edges at all (in which case, skip steps 4–6).

you will need • selection of fabrics (to work out amounts, use steps 1, 4, and 7) • matching thread • 2¾yd/2.5m of ¼in-/5mm-wide piping cord (optional) • 24in/60cm square pillow • sewing machine • ruler, scissors, pins

1 For the front, cut out 16 patches, each exactly 7in/17cm square. Arrange the patches attractively, ensuring two patches in the same fabric are not side by side. Make a note of the arrangement on a piece of paper, or chalk a number indicating the position on the wrong side of each patch.

2 Starting at the left of the top row, place the second patch on top of the first patch, right sides together. Pin together along the right-hand edge, and stitch a ½in/1cm seam. Open out the patches. Place the third patch on top of the second, and stitch together in the same way. Repeat to join the fourth patch to the third one. Do the same for the remaining three rows. Press all seams open.

3 Place the second row on top of the first row, right sides together, lining up the seams. Pin together along the lower edge, making sure seams are aligned and all seam allowances are flat. Stitch a ½in/1cm seam. Open out the patches, place the third row on top of the second, and stitch together in the same way. Repeat to join the fourth row to the third one. Press all seams open. This completes the front.

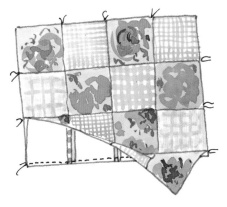

4 If you want to pipe the edges, you'll need a 2¾yd/2.5m length of bias binding. To make your own, cut 1½in-/3.5cm-wide strips of fabric on the diagonal, and stitch together at the ends, right sides together as shown, until the strip is long enough. Press open the seams and trim off the points.

5 Right side out, wrap the bias binding around the cord. With raw edges of the binding even, pin near the cord. Using the machine piping foot or zipper foot, baste close to the cord. Pin the piping to the right side of the front around the edges, starting in the center of one side— the basting on the piping should be just within the seam allowance, as shown. At the corners, clip into the piping seam allowances.

6 With the piping foot or zipper foot, baste along the piping basting line, leaving 2in/5cm unstitched at each end. Unpick the basting on the piping at these ends so you can pull back the bias binding. Trim the cord so the ends butt up, then wrap the bias binding around the cord, turning under ¼in/5mm on the overlapping end. Baste to the front.

7 For the back, cut out two pieces measuring 25in/62cm x 16in/39cm from one of the fabrics. Turn under a narrow double hem on one long edge of each back piece; pin and stitch. Overlap the two pieces and, right sides together, place them on the front as shown, so that the raw edges are even. Pin around all four sides.

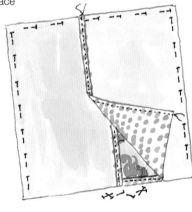

8 With the piping foot or zipper foot still on the machine, stitch through all four layers, very close to the piping so the basting will be hidden within the seam allowance. (Or, if you are not using piping, stitch a ½in/1cm seam using the regular presser foot on the machine.) Trim off the corners of the seam allowances. Turn the cover right side out and press. Insert the pillow through the opening.

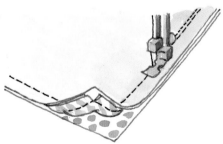

TIP *To align seams perfectly, try to cut each patch to exactly the same size, and ensure that all seams are exactly the same width.*

button lampshade

This lampshade provides a novel way to use the contents of your buttonbox. You can use buttons in all colors of the rainbow, as shown here, coordinate them to match the room, or for a more elegant look, limit your selection to cream and white, perhaps interspersing them with mother-of-pearl buttons. Old lampshades can often be found in charity shops and thrift stores—all you need is one to complement the size of the lamp stand itself. If you wish, you could add a row of beads to the bottom of the frame, suspending them on short lengths of wire.

you will need • old lampshade frame • sandpaper or wire wool (optional) • good selection of buttons • reel of fine wire • scissors or wirecutters

1 If re-using an old lampshade, first strip off the old fabric. If necessary, rub down the metal frame with sandpaper or metal wool to remove any paint. Sort the buttons into piles according to their size. The smallest buttons are used at the top edge of the shade, and they gradually increase in size toward the base of the shade.

2 Cut a long length of wire from the reel and wrap one end securely around the base of the frame.

3 Thread one of the largest buttons onto the wire, pushing it down level with the bottom of the frame. Thread on more buttons, gradually decreasing in size until you have a threaded length of wire long enough to reach the top edge of the frame.

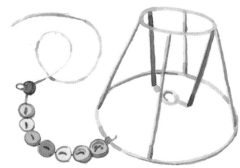

4 At the top edge, wrap the wire securely around the frame several times, making sure that it is pulled taut. Starting at the top, thread another row of buttons, this time working from the smallest to the largest. Wrap the threaded wire around the base of the frame. Continue threading the wire until you have enough rows of buttons to complete the lampshade. Wrap the wire around the frame to secure, then cut off any excess.

padded headboard

This fabric-covered padded headboard is simple and inexpensive to make, yet it will add both comfort and sophistication to a bed. The size of the headboard means you could choose a bold, large-scale pattern, but a subtly textured fabric will also look great, as shown here. The instructions show you how to make the headboard by covering MDF or plywood with foam and then fabric, or you could adapt the technique to cover an existing headboard with new fabric. If making the headboard from scratch, you can easily adjust the height or change the shape. The headboard sits on legs, which can be bolted to the bed frame if you wish.

you will need • paper for patterns • ¾in/2cm MDF or plywood, cut to shape (see step 1)
• 1½in/4cm polyurethane foam, cut to shape (see step 2) • white glue • decorator fabric
• ruler, scissors, heavy-duty stapler, and ½in/1cm staples • drill and bolts (optional)

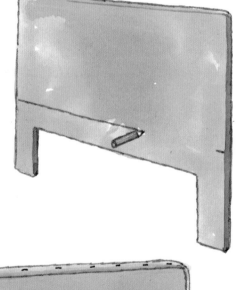

1 The MDF or plywood should be the same width as your bed frame and a height of about 36in/91cm from the bottom of the mattress, with top corners rounded off slightly. The legs, which are cut as one piece with the headboard, should be 10in/25cm wide and a height equal to the distance from the floor to the bottom of the mattress. If you want to bolt the legs to the bed frame (see step 4), make sure that the legs line up with the holes in the bed frame, and adjust their position if necessary.

Make a paper pattern and have the piece cut to shape. Check the fit against the bed, and draw a line where the top of the mattress will come to.

2 Make a second paper pattern of the headboard without the legs. The width should be the width of the headboard plus 3in/8cm. For the height, measure from the top of the headboard down to the mattress line and add 1½in/4cm. Buy the foam cut to shape. Glue the foam to the front of the headboard, lining up the bottom edge with the mattress line. Wrap the foam over the top and sides and staple along these edges.

3 Cut a rectangle of fabric about 6in/15cm wider and deeper than the headboard (excluding the legs). If it has a pattern, make sure the design will be centered and any vertical or horizontal lines will be parallel to the edges.

Place the fabric on a flat surface, wrong side up, and center the headboard on it, foam side down. Wrap the fabric over the sides and on to the back of the headboard, stretching it taut and folding it neatly at the corners. Staple in place. Clip into the fabric at the legs as shown, to allow the fabric to be wrapped to the back between the legs.

4 Cut two more rectangles of fabric, each the height of the leg plus 1in/2cm, and 21in/51cm wide. On each, press under ½in/1cm on the top and bottom edges and on one side edge. Wrap the fabric around each leg, with the finished side edge covering the raw side edge, and staple in place.

For the back, cut a rectangle of fabric the same size as the headboard. Press under ½in/1cm on all four edges, and staple to the back around these edges, covering the raw edges of the decorator fabric. If desired, drill holes in the legs to match the holes in the bed frame, and bolt them together.

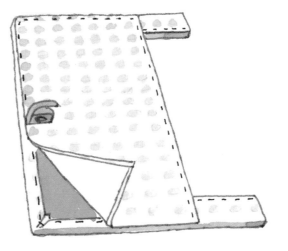

new cover for director's chair

The director's chair never goes out of style, as its classic design makes it equally suited to the contemporary living room, the rustic kitchen, or outdoors on the patio, deck, or balcony. Often an old one is too well loved and sturdy to throw out, but may nevertheless have started to look decidedly shabby, with a faded or worn-out seat and back. Replacing these elements is surprisingly easy and will give the chair a whole new lease on life. Be sure to choose a strong fabric such as heavyweight canvas—or you could use one or two small, thin woven rag rugs.

you will need • sturdy fabric • matching strong thread • tape measure, craft knife (optional), ruler, pins, scissors, sewing machine (if using fabric rather than a rug) • furniture tacks and hammer, or heavy-duty stapler and staples • large grommets and grommet-setting tool (grommets must be big enough for the bolts or screws used in the back rails)

1 To work out the width of the new back piece, measure the width of the old fabric back, including the wraparound for each rail. If using fabric, add 2in/5cm (but not if you are using a rug). For the depth, measure the old back, and add 2in/5cm if using fabric. (If using a rug, add 1in/2.5cm to the depth only if one edge will be an unfinished edge—see step 2.) Do the same for the seat.

If the old fabric is badly stretched, it may be easier to measure the frame instead. Study how the old fabric back and seat have been attached to the chair, and then remove them, cutting away the fabric with a craft knife if necessary.

2 Cut out the new seat and back to the above dimensions. (If using a rug, try to place the finished edges where there will be the most wear, such as at the front of the seat.)

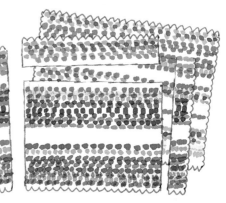

3 If using fabric, zigzag stitch the raw edges and then press under a 1in/2.5cm hem on the top and bottom edges of the back and on the back and front edges of the seat; stitch each hem with two rows of stitching. Also press under a 1in/2.5cm hem on the side edges of both fabric pieces, but do not stitch these side hems, as you may need to adjust them. (If using a rug, turn under a 1in/2.5cm hem on an unfinished top or bottom edge of the back, and/or unfinished back edge of the seat; hand sew in place. Do not turn under side hems if using a rug.)

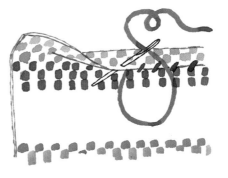

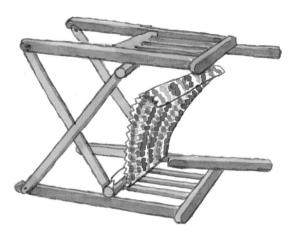

4 To attach the seat, lay the chair on one side and wrap one side edge of the seat over one rail, with the folded edge (unfolded edge if using a rug) on the underside of the rail and parallel to it. Secure with tacks or staples. Lay the chair on its other side and repeat for the other side edge of the seat and other rail, using only a few tacks or staples. Check the fit, adjust if necessary, and then secure with more tacks or staples.

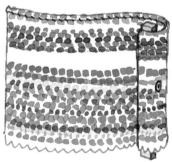

5 For the back, take out any bolts or screws in the rails and remove the rails from the chair frame. (If there aren't any bolts or screws, there is no need to remove the rails.) Wrap one side edge of the back around one rail, with the edge on the rear inside.

To make holes in the back for any bolts or screws, mark on the fabric the positions that correspond to each hole in the rail, then insert grommets in the back at the marked positions. Repeat for the other side edge of the back and other side rail, checking the fit and adjusting if necessary before inserting grommets.

6 To attach the back, secure one side edge to the rail with tacks or staples, being careful to match any grommets to the ends of the hole in the rail. Repeat for the other side edge.

7 If necessary, reassemble the chair by putting the rails back into the chair frame and refitting the bolts or screws.

ultra-simple curtain

You could hardly find a simpler curtain than this—it must be the ultimate in contemporary chic. Use either a piece of unbleached muslin, as in the photograph, or a panel of antique linen if it is the right size for your window. The top is folded over a curtain wire, creating a generous integral valance, and the clothespins stop the curtain from slipping off. If you want to open it, simply unclip the clothespins and take it down. Or, for a similar look with a pair of panels that open and close, fold over the tops and then use clip-on rings to attach them to a curtain wire or narrow metal rod.

you will need • unbleached muslin or linen • matching thread • scissors, pins, needle or sewing machine (optional) • curtain wire with 2 eyelets and 2 cup hooks • mini wooden clothespins

1 Measure the window and decide where the top of the curtain will be. Also decide the depth of the integral valance. Add these two measurements together, and also add 2in/4cm for hems—the total is the length of the fabric panel.

For the width, add a little to the window width to allow the curtain to hang softly (the amount of fullness is up to you), and also add 2in/4cm for hems. Cut the fabric to these dimensions.

2 If using a panel of antique linen that does not need cutting to make it fit, you will not need to hem the edges. Otherwise, turn under a double ½in/1cm hem on all raw edges (do not press), pin or baste, and stitch in place.

3 Cut the length of wire to fit the window opening, and screw an eyelet into each end of the wire. Stretch the wire a little, and mark on the window frame where the two cup hooks need to be. Screw the hooks into the frame at the marked positions, and hook an eyelet over each. If the wire is not taut, you may need to remove one eyelet and trim the end of the wire slightly before replacing the eyelet. Drape the fabric panel over the wire, and hold it in place with the clothespins.

button-decorated jars

Glass jars come in some nice shapes and useful sizes, so it's a great pity not to make use of them when the contents are used up. Decorating the jars can make them look special enough to use in the kitchen or workroom as containers for wooden spoons or other utensils, paintbrushes, pencils, rulers, scissors, and so on, or to use as votive holders indoors or outside. Often the simplest, most rustic decoration is the most effective, such as these ivory-colored buttons strung onto the rims of the jars with wire.

you will need • glass jars • spools of thick wire and thin wire • selection of buttons • wirecutters or scissors

1 Cut a piece of thick wire long enough to wrap around the rim of the jar twice, allowing enough extra to secure the wire. Wrap the wire loosely around the rim of the jar, without fastening it.

2 Cut a short length of fine wire and use it to attach a button to the wire encircling the jar, rather like sewing on a button. You don't need to tie knots—just twist the end of the fine wire around and around the other end. Repeat to attach buttons all the way around.

3 If you want to create a wire handle, cut another piece of thick wire and attach one end to each side of the wire encircling the rim, twisting each end to secure it. Wire more buttons to this handle if desired.

4 Now pull the ends of the thick wire to tighten it around the jar rim, and secure the ends by twisting them together.

designed by Sania Pell

knitted patch throw

This is a really easy throw to knit—all you need to be able to do is cast on, knit, and cast off. It's also a great way to use up odds and ends of yarns from your stash, or raid friend's stashes: keen knitters will often be only too glad to give embarrassingly large overspills of yarn to a good home. It's best to use yarns that are all more or less the same thickness or you will have problems making all the squares the same size. For a warm yet lightweight throw, double-knitting yarn is the best thickness to choose.

you will need • selection of yarns in different colors • knitting needles • pins • tapestry needle

1 Using knitting needles the right size for the yarn you have chosen (check on the yarn ball band to see what size is recommended), cast on 40 stitches. Work in garter stitch (knitting every row) until the piece of knitting is square, then cast off. Count how many rows you knitted and knit every square the same size. Knit enough squares to make a throw the desired size.

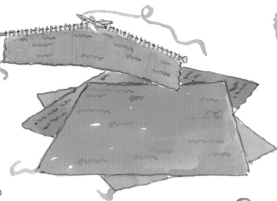

2 Pin two squares together along the row-end edges; garter stitch is reversible so you don't need to worry about right and wrong sides.

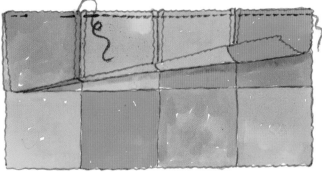

3 Thread the tapestry needle with a length of yarn. The color doesn't matter as the stitches will not show on the right side of the throw. Using ordinary backstitch, sew the squares together along the pinned edge.

4 To secure the ends of yarn make a couple of backstitches over one another at the start and finish of the seam. Weave the ends of yarn into the seam for a neat finish. Continue pinning and sewing squares together until the strip of squares is the desired width of the throw. Make as many strips as you need in this way. Pin and sew the strips together to make the throw, matching the squares so that they line up in rows in both directions.

fabric doorstop

Traditional French ticking makes for a chic yet practical doorstop that's also simple to sew. You could use a heavy canvas, denim recycled from a pair of jeans, or even corduroy fabric if you prefer. As long as the fabric has a tight weave and is fairly robust, it will work well.

you will need • pins • one 10in/25cm length of ¾-in/2-cm wide cotton webbing or heavy tape • two 6¾ x 3¼in/17 x 8cm strips, two 8½ x 3¼in/22 x 8cm strips, and two 6¾ x 8½in/17 x 22cm rectangles of ticking fabric • sewing machine • strong sewing thread • iron • large spoon • builders' sand • hand-sewing needle

1 Positioning it centrally on one short end, pin 2in/5cm of one end of the cotton webbing to the right side of one of the smaller strips of ticking. Pin 2in/5cm of the other end of the webbing to the other end of the strip. Set the sewing machine to a small straight stitch and sew a square around the pinned ends of the webbing to sew them to the ticking. Sew about ⅛in/3mm in from the edge of the webbing and sew over the lines of stitching twice for strength.

2 Right-sides facing, pin one end of each longer strip of ticking to each end of the short piece. Machine-sew the ends together, taking a ½in/1cm seam allowance. Pin and sew the remaining short strip to the free end of one of the long strips. Press all the seam allowances open.

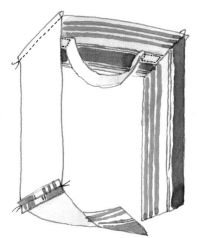

3 Right-sides facing, pin the joined strips of ticking to one of the rectangular pieces, matching the seams in the strip to the corners of the rectangle. Taking a ½in/1cm seam allowance, sew the strip to the rectangle, pivoting at the corners for a neat finish. Pin the other rectangle to the free edge of the strip and sew the seam in the same way.

4 Turn the bag right-side out through the gap in the side strip, which should be on the bottom. Turn under and finger-press a ½in/1cm seam allowance on each side of the gap. Spoon sand through the gap into the bag until the bag is about three-quarters full. Using the hand-sewing needle and small, firm stitches, oversew the gap closed.

painted display cabinet

Gently distressed paint in muted shades of soft gray and off-white have turned a heavy, dark wood armoire into a smart Gustavian-style display cabinet. Large pieces of dark wood furniture can seem oppressive and ponderous in contemporary interiors, but if painted in light colors and subtly distressed to maintain the vintage look, they can look positively delicate. In addition, the hints of dark wood showing through the distressed areas add just enough definition to stop the colors from being insipid. Other soft pastels that would work in the same way include shades of creamy straw yellow, cool blues, and blue-grays, or dusky pinks, all of which were used in Gustavian homes.

you will need • steel wool • proprietary varnish stripper (optional) • fine sandpaper • undercoat
• flat latex or emulsion paint in cream, dove gray, gray-green, and off-white • decorator's brushes
• low-tack masking tape

1 Depending on the condition of the wood, either rub down all the surfaces with steel wool and proprietary varnish stripper to remove old varnish and polish, or simply wash it with a solution of strong detergent and rinse with clean water afterward.

Sand the surface with fine sandpaper, working with the grain, to provide a key for the paint. Wipe thoroughly with a clean cloth. Remove the shelves (if possible) and paint the top, bottom, and front of each with undercoat and two coats of cream paint, allowing it to dry between coats. Paint the rest of the interior in the same way.

2 Use masking tape to protect any vulnerable areas, pressing it down firmly and clipping into it to shape it around curves. Apply undercoat to the exterior. When dry, paint the main parts of the exterior with two coats of dove gray paint, again allowing it to dry between coats.

Depending on the design of the cabinet, paint selected areas with gray-green instead of dove gray. When the second coat is touch-dry, carefully remove any masking tape adjacent to painted areas.

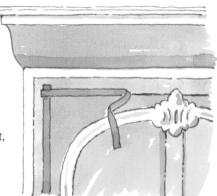

3 Pick out detailing—such as the feet and the moldings on the cornice, on the drawer, and around the window and door—in two coats of off-white paint, using a small brush. Do not overload the brush with paint. Allow to dry after each coat, removing any masking tape when the second coat is touch-dry.

4 In places that would be subject to wear, particularly on edges and the areas painted off-white, use steel wool or sandpaper to distress (rub away) the paint a little, allowing the dark wood to show through. Clean the brushes in warm soapy water, rinse, and dry.

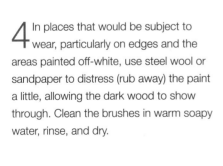

TIP *If you like the chalky look of antique paint, you could use calcimine rather than flat latex or emulsion paint.*

striped stairway

Colorful painted stripes provide a modern take on the traditional stair runner and allow you to update your stairway at a fraction of the price of a new carpet while giving it a fun, upbeat look. The key to this treatment is varying the widths and colors of the stripes, which are painted in straight lines through the use of masking tape. Antique white paint used as a background for the stripes reflects light and brightens up the long, narrow stairway without looking harsh. Bear in mind that you won't be able to use the stairs until the paint is completely dry.

you will need • knot sealer (optional), sandpaper • wood primer (optional), undercoat • eggshell or floor paint in white and selection of colors, such as dark green, medium green, light green, pale pink, and black • polyurethane varnish and brush (optional) • mineral spirits • decorators' paintbrushes • fine artists' brush• ruler and light pencil • 1in-/2.5cm-wide low-tack masking tape

1 Prepare the surface first by sanding smooth with sandpaper. Sweep or vacuum thoroughly, and then wipe with a clean cloth soaked in mineral spirits. Apply primer if the wood is bare, and treat any knots with knot sealer. When dry, apply undercoat. Leave it to dry and then apply two coats of the white paint, allowing it to dry after each coat.

2 Measure and mark out the stripes lightly in pencil. For ease of painting, the pale pink stripes between the green stripes need to be at least 1in/2.5cm (the width of the tape). Mask outside both edges of each dark, medium, and light green stripe, as shown. Press the edges of the tape down firmly.

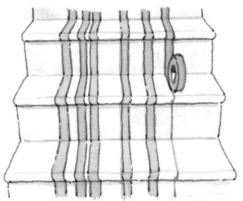

3 Kneeling on the fourth step from the top, paint the masked stripes on the top three steps, including the risers. Use brushes that are about the same width as the stripes. It's easiest to use one for each color, so you won't have to keep cleaning them. Avoid overloading the brush with paint. Leave the paint to dry completely, then apply a second coat. When this is touch-dry, carefully peel off the strips of tape and throw them away (don't try to reuse).

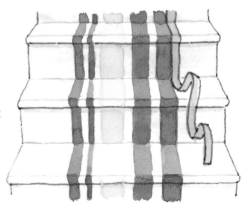

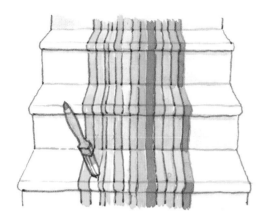

4 Move down to kneel on the seventh step from the top and paint the fourth, fifth, and sixth steps in the same way. Continue down the stairway until all the masked stripes are painted. Now go back and repeat the process for the pale pink stripes—it's fine to mask over painted areas once they are dry. Finally, after removing the tape, paint the thin black lines (masking them if you prefer).

After all the paint has dried overnight, use a fine artist's brush to touch up any feathered edges. Finally, unless you have used floor paint, apply at least three coats of varnish, allowing it to dry between coats. Clean the brushes in mineral spirits and then soapy water (or just soapy water if the paint is water-based).

TIP *Paintwork on stairs will inevitably become scuffed and worn, so it's best to regard the distressed, shabby chic look as part of the charm of this treatment. Varnish helps prevent the need to repaint too often, or you could use a floor paint. This is tough and hard-wearing, comes in a range of colors, and does not need varnishing.*

useful addresses

As well as all the markets listed below, look for local antiques markets and auctions in telephone directories, tourist information centers, and in the local press. Also, many homeware stores either have online clearance stores or "sale" sections, or you can check their websites for their factory outlets.

US

American Park 'n' Swap, Arizona
The largest open-air flea market in the southwest
www.americanparknswap.com

Ann Arbor Antiques Market, Michigan
Exhibitors offer a wide range of antiques covering all the major eras
www.annarborantiquesmarket.com

Annex/Hell's Kitchen
Flea Market, New York
New York's most famous flea market
www.hellskitchenfleamarket.com

The Antique Shopping Guide
An excellent resource for locating your nearest antique store
www.antiqueshoppingguide.com

Brimfield Flea Market, Massachusetts
New England's biggest outdoor antiques fair
www.brimfield.com

Canton First Monday Trade Days, Texas
These monthly events attract up to 7,000 vendors
www.firstmondaycanton.com

Chicago Antique Market, Illinois
High-quality goods are on offer in the Randolph Street Market District
www.chicagoantiquemarket.com

Ebay
Needs no introduction. The world's biggest online auction site—perfect for antique hunting
www.ebay.com

Find A Flea Market.
Great site dedicated to helping you find local flea markets
www.findafleamarket.com

Flea USA
Gives listings by state of flea markets
www.fleausa.com

Fleaworld, Florida
A large flea market located in Orlando
www.fleaworld.com

Goodridge Guides
A useful calendar of events tells you where to find your next flea market
www.goodridgeguides.com

Long Beach Antique Market, California
One of the best flea markets in Los Angeles
www.longbeachantiquemarket.com

Q Flea
An online antiques auction site
www.qflea.com

Scott Antique Markets
Large shows in Atlanta and Ohio
www.scottantiquemarket.com

Stewart Promotions
Promoters of quality flea markets in Kentucky, Indiana, and Tennessee
www.stewartpromotions.com

Wholesale Distributors
Website aimed at wholesalers but gives list of the largest flea markets in the US
www.wholesaledistributorsnet.com

UK

ANTIQUES MARKETS

Alfie's Antique Market, London
One of London's best markets that is loved by collectors across the globe
www.alfiesantiques.com

Antiques.co.uk
Guide to UK dealers with useful advice on periods
www.antiques.co.uk

Antiques Atlas
The UK location-based antiques directory and online catalogue listing shops, fairs, and auction houses
www.antiques-atlas.com

Antiques News
Great website with up-to-date news on fairs and the UK antiques trade
www.antiquesnews.co.uk

Bermondsey Market
Bermondsey Square, London SE11
Fridays, 5am-2pm

British Antique Dealers' Association
www.bada.org

DMG Antiques Fairs
Organizers of the UK's premier antiques and collectors fairs at Shepton Mallet, Newark, Ardingly, and Detling
www.dmgantiquefairs.com

Gray's Antiques Market, London
Home to a diverse collection of books, jewelry, antiques, and fashion
www.graysantiques.com

Kempton Park Racecourse
Hosts a large antique market twice monthly
www.kemptonantiques.com

Kent Country Auctions
14 West St, Faversham, ME13 7JE
01795 590174

P & A Antiques
Organizers of specialist antique fairs with sellers offering vintage fashions, accessories, and textiles
www.pa-antiques.co.uk

Portobello Road Antiques Market, London
The world-famous flea market
www.portobelloroad.co.uk

Squires Antiques, Kent
A fantastic trader with over 25 years' experience
www.squiresantiques.com

Street Sensation
Guide to London's markets
www.streetsensation.co.uk

Swinderby Antiques Fair, Lincolnshire
One of the UK's largest antiques fairs
www.arthurswallowfairs.co.uk

Trouver Antiques
Based in France but with twice yearly sales in Britain
www.trouverantiques.co.uk

HOMESTORES WITH GOOD BASIC RANGES
B&Q: *www.diy.com*
IKEA: *www.ikea.com*
Sofa.com: *www.sofa.com*
Laura Ashley:
www.lauraashley.com
Debenhams:
www.debenhams.com
BHS: *www.bhs.com*

MODERN FURNITURE STORES
The Conran Shop:
www.ConranShop.co.uk
IKEA: *www.ikea.com*
Habitat *www. habitat.co.uk*

OTHER FURNITURE
Sasha Waddell
Scandinavian-inspired painted furniture
www.sashawaddell.com

Dormy House
Unpainted furniture
www.thedormyhouse.com

CHINA AND GLASS
Bombay Duck
www.bombayduck.com

Graham & Greene
www.grahamandgreen.co.uk

FABRICS AND BEDLINEN
Cath Kidston
www.cathkidston.co.uk

Stitch Design Works
www.stitchdesignworks.co.uk

CLEARANCE STORES
TK Maxx
Top designer brands which don't have their own sales or clearance shops supply TK Maxx (*www.tkmaxx.com*) and its sister brand (*www.homesense.com*) with seconds, discontinued lines, cancelled orders, and surplus stock. New items arrive each week, so check regularly.

The Good Deal Directory
Listing of factory shops and discount warehouses
www.gooddealdirectory.co.uk

PAINTS
Farrow & Ball
Historic paints
www.farrow-ball.com

The Paint Library
www.paintlibrary.co.uk

Dulux
www.dulux.co.uk

Marston & Langinger
www.marston-and-langinger.com

MISCELLANEOUS
Hoyle Iron Foundry
Iron brackets
www.ironheritage.co.uk

Lou Rota
Decoupage chairs and "bug" china
www.lourota.com

M&F Products
Lampshade frames
01435 810451

Random Retail
www.randomretail.co.uk

Shelf Store
www.shelfstore.co.uk

Trip Trap
Soft lyewood soap from Danecare
www.danecare.co.uk

LOCATIONS
The Albion at Deal, Kent
(featured on pages 58–63) is available for holiday lets.
www.lightlocations.com

index

*Note: Page numbers in **bold** refer to Projects*

authors' acknowledgments

A big thank you to Simon Brown whose beautiful photographs perfectly capture the ideas behind this book. Many thanks to all the kind friends who allowed us to photograph their homes and to all the new people we met who generously welcomed us into their houses. Thank you to stylists Clare Nash and Sarah Charles. Finally, thank you to the team at Cico Books—Cindy Richards, Sally Powell, Gillian Haslam, and Christine Wood.